Insider Trading: Profit from

Tony Pow

Why you invest

You will need to learn about investing sooner or later in your life. You also need to take some calculated risks.

Compare the returns of the following assets: cash, CDs, treasury bills, bonds, real estate and stocks. We start with the risk-free investments and end with the riskiest. It turns out that the average returns are in the opposite order. Cash and CDs are not risk-free as inflation eats our profits. For example, the real return is negative for the 2% return in a CD and a 3% inflation rate. In addition, you have to pay taxes for the 'returns'. <u>Our capitalist system punishes us for not taking risks</u>. However, protect your portfolio such as using stop orders and not using leverages including options for beginners. Start being a turtle investor rather than a trader that could <u>lose</u> all your money.

There are two kinds of risk: blind risk and calculated risk. If you buy a stock due to a recommendation from a commentator on TV or a tip, most likely you are taking a blind risk. It would be the same in buying a house without thoroughly evaluating the house and its neighborhood. When you buy stocks with a proven strategy (i.e., when/what stocks to buy and when/what stocks to sell), you are taking a calculated risk. In the long run, stocks with calculated and educated risks are profitable.

Be a turtle investor by investing in value stocks and holding for longer time periods (a year or more). "Buy and Monitor" is a better approach than "Buy and Hold" as some could lose all the stocks' value such as in the failure of Enron.

For experienced investors, shorting, short-term trading and covered calls would make you good profits. Simple market timing would reduce your losses during market downturns. If you buy a market ETF and use my simple market timing, you should have beaten the market by a wide margin from 2000 to 2019.

With so many fraudulent and poor managed hedge funds (but many exceptions), do not trust anyone with your investing. Do not buy investing instruments that are highly marketed such as annuity and term insurance.

If you are a handy man and do not mind to satisfy the constant requests of your tenants, buy real estate in growing areas that could be very profitable in the long run. Take advantage of the tax laws such as investing in a 401K especially the part that is matched by your company and/or a Roth IRA.

Why you trust me

This book represents my years of investing experience, the hundreds of investing books I read and thousands of simulations. Hopefully this book will improve your financial health substantially as it has one to mine. I also hope that by reading this book you can become a better investor no matter if you are a **beginner or a fund manager**.

My children have no interest in investing, so I do not hold back anything. I expect my readers will do better financially if they can avoid my mistakes that I will point out in this book. Today and at my age I am a very conservative investor and am doing well with my investments. I wish I could have tried out many of my strategies earlier in my investing life.

- I had a 50% return in one month in 2018 by using my year-end strategy. I would challenge any investor with this type of monthly return in a diversified portfolio of 8 stocks or more.

- I recommended 20 stocks in an article titled Amazing Return in Seeking Alpha. If you bought them on the published date, you would have beaten the S&P 500 index by more than 100% in a year without considering dividends as demonstrated in my other article A Tale of Two Portfolios.

    I challenge anyone who has a better one-year performance by recommending a diversified portfolio of 15 or more stocks in any publication.

- In 01/2016, I recommended buying OIL in my posts in Seeking Alpha's Wall Street Breakfast and my blog when oil was less than $30 per barrel.
http://tonyp4idea.blogspot.com/2016/01/oil-price.html.

- Recommended Apple at $55.72 (1-7 split adjusted) on April 19, 2013 as the only example in my book Scoring Stocks and I recommended selling it at $132 in 2/2015 with valid arguments described in this link.
http://tonyp4idea.blogspot.com/2015/02/dump-apple.html

My amazing returns

Amazing Returns

To achieve a consistent 10% return above S&P 500 over many years is every fund manager's dream. To double one's investment above the S&P 500 return is amazing while tripling it is unheard of. I beat the S&P 500 by 700% and I can detail the history of my transactions.

Many analysts show their average yearly returns and/or their returns of their top 10 stocks this time of year. The market has closed early today on Christmas Eve, so I have the time to check my recent performance. As a trader with many trades, it would be far too complicated for me to do the same for the entire year. I selected all the stocks I purchased in the last 90 days. Most of them are deeply-valued stocks. Let's check how I performed so far on these stocks.

Whenever you have achieved a high return such as this one, take the profit as it may have reached its peaks. To me, most profits are made in swing trades with an average holding period of just 90 days.

Stocks bought and their returns as of 12/25/12

Stocks	Date Bought	Return	SPY Return
BANR	12/07/12	3%	-.13%
KTCC	12/06/12	0%	.7%
QCOR	12/07/12	15%	-.1%
KTCC	12/06/12	-1%	.7%
ACTV	12/05/12	-5%	.7%
IAG	12/05/12	-1%	.7%
ADES	12/04/12	6%	.6%
NC	12/03/12	15%	-.3%
VELT	12/03/12	64%	-.3%
ANR	11/28/12	33%	4.8%
AAPL	11/16/12	1%	4.8%
C	11/14/12	13%	3.0%
DECK	11/13/12	16%	2.7%
MSFT	11/13/12	0%	2.7%
ALU	11/13/12	38%	2.7%
DLTR	11/09/12	7%	3.4%
CAT	11/08/12	4%	1.9%
MSFT	11/07/12	-8%	.5%
BSX	10/24/12	14%	.3%
BSX	10/19/12	7%	.3%

20			
AVG:		11%	1.35%

Beat SPY (in %) = (11%-1.35%)/1.35% = 716% or 7 times

Average Return = averaging each return of 20 stocks = 11%
Average Annualized Return = 148% or 122% (= 11% *365 / avg. holding period)
Average Return = Profit / Capitalization   = 10%[1]

How the returns are calculated

Using BANR to illustrate how the return and the SPY return are calculated.

BANR	12/07/12	3%	-.13%

BANR was bought on 12/07/12 (17 days from 12/24/12) at 27.93 and it was at 30.43 on 12/24/12.
Rate of Return = (30.43 – 27.93) / 27.93 = 3%

SPY was at 142.53 on 12/07/12 and at 142.35 on 12/24/12.
  Rate of Return = (142.35-142.53) / 142.53 = -.13%

Commissions and dividends are not included for simplicity. Commissions are negligible and dividends could add about another 2% for the annual returns.

Interpreting the performance results

The quantity of each stock bought is not important as I am comparing the return of the stock. However, a few stocks have been listed twice as I bought two times usually on separate dates. If I chose them as one purchase instead of two, my return would appear even better. The purchases are real, so the amount of each stock is not identical to each other.

I'm not too excited yet. This phenomenal return could be just this one time only. 90 days is a short period. Consistency could be achieved with an improved stock picking technique, plain luck or a combination. By any measure, it is an extremely decent return. However, I do not expect beating S&P 500 by 7 times again.

My best return is from 2009 in my largest taxable account. It was over 80% beating the SPY by about 3 times. 2003 is another good year for profit. These two years are defined by me as the Early Recovery stage in a market cycle and the market provides the best profit opportunity.

The four losers are MSFT (-8%), ACTV (-5%), KTCC (-1%) and IAG (-1%). The best winners are: VELT (64%), ALU (38%), ANR (33%) and QCOR (19%). The following are in a 14% to 16% range: DECK, NC and BSX (2 purchases). Click here for the entire list.

Cheating the results

I could 'cheat' for better results by doing the following, but I did not:

1. Exclude stocks only purchased in last 20 days (instead of 15).

2. If my purchases of CSCO were included, the result would be even better. CSCO has been bought three times on 7/24/12 and it has gained 31% as of 12/25/12. I still have CSCO, but it is not included as it just hit the 90-days requirement.

3. I could include those buy orders that had not been executed due to their fast appreciation.

Hence, there are many ways to cheat, so you should read others' results carefully.

What stocks were included

There were 20 purchases. I bought some stocks twice and that counted as two purchases. None of the stocks have been sold as of 12/25/12. I have excluded the stocks that I am testing a strategy by trading them every month and most are in a separate account.

How the stocks were picked

The majority of the stocks were screened by my selected screens that had been proven profitable in the last 3 to 6 months, or are historically profitable at this stage of the market cycle. I also analyzed most of the screened stocks and assigned a score (15 and higher is a buy) based on the metrics that had a reliable prediction recently. I do not stick with the scoring system 100% of the time, but most of them stocks that I purchased twice have high scores.

The poor performers were scored as: MSFT with a score of 13, ACTV 16, KTCC 27 and IAG 23. The scoring system is OK. MSFT should not be bought judging from its low score. However, I believe MSFT has a long-term appreciation potential. The other three are the latest purchases in this portfolio and they may perform better in a longer period of time.

The winners were scored as: VELT 34, ALU was not scored, ANR was not scored and QCOR 30. The scoring system is great for this group. ALU and ANR were selected from two Seeking Alpha articles and their selections were not based on these scores. I read several Wall Street Journal articles on ALU and CSCO to convince myself to buy both of them.

The average winners were scored as follows: DECK 9, NC 26 and BSX was not scored. DECK was selected based on an article from Seeking Alpha and it seemed DECK was experiencing the same short squeeze as CROX once did. BSX was selected from a Sunday paper article.

Observations

1. I notice that most big winners (ALU is $1) have a stock price less than $10. The myth of holding quality stocks with prices higher than $15 is not true here as most of my big winners were below $10 including ALU.

2. I did not double my normal purchases on VELT and ALU, which both turned out to be my best performers. VELT scored high in my analysis. ALU was very convincing but it seemed to be risky. 'Nothing risk and nothing gained' applies here. I did triple my purchase on CSCO, which is a large company with good fundamentals that were not yet 'discovered' by the market.

   Both AAPL and DECK gained more than 25% and then lost most of their gains during my short holding period. I should have sold AAPL as many of my fellow investors sold the winners expecting higher capital gains taxes next year. The myth of 'buy and hold' does not work here.

3. During this period, I had several buy orders that were not executed due to their rising stock prices. Market orders could be the solution. It is another example of pennies smart and a pound foolish.

4. It will be interesting to check the results again in 6 and 12 months. Except ALU, all are in my taxable accounts and I usually keep them for a year to qualify for the lower tax rates due to capital gains.

5. I have not described any specific method, but these concepts help you to build better strategies to customize to your individual situations and/or market conditions. Invest the money you can afford to lose. Past performance does not guarantee future results.

6. Reading articles such as Seeking Alpha can be beneficial providing they are not 'bump-and-switch' scheme. However, you should do your own analysis. It is your money after all.

7. The market has been up by .8% in the last 90 days and this portfolio increased by 11%. If my portfolio amplifies the market, I wonder whether it will be down by the same rate in a down market.
8. This portfolio is quite diversified even that I have not planned that way except weighing more with high tech companies. There are no big winners and no big losers that could change the average returns.
9. I tried not to include emerging countries such as China as I do not trust their balance sheets.
10. I have never achieved such an amazing return. I'm emotionally detached to big wins and big losses. It could be plain luck. Even the best strategy will have its "black swan" moment eventually.
11. To achieve over 100% annualized return is not sustainable by checking the top performers of the S&P 500 index and their returns. However, it is possible but not likely if you churn your portfolio more than once and you time the market correctly.
12. Time to take profits as most stocks here have achieved my objectives. Use the cash to buy stocks with a similar appreciation potential. You will never go broke taking profits.

Conclusion

My three steps of making a stock purchase are: 1. Market timing, 2. Screening stocks, 3. Stock Analysis and 4. When and what to sell. They have all been discussed throughout the book. Market timing and strategy (#2 and #3) does not always work, but it will go better with using them.

I am the living proof *against* the Efficiency Theory and the claims that stock picking does not work. It may not work from time to time, but in the long run it works.

Footnote

[1] Profit / Capitalization should be a little less than 20%. The original 10% is correct when you invest all the 20 stocks at the start of the beginning of the investment period. I bought these stocks on different dates. If I assume the average time of all the stock purchases is at a mid-point, then my average capitalization is only half and hence giving a 20% return.

It is slightly less than 20% as I did not include the stocks that I bought in the last 15 days. Use the number for a comparison and that's why we have to be concerned with the performance from most investment subscriptions.

Introduction

Following the insider purchases could be very profitable. No one knows the company and the sector better than the insiders of the company.

The following represent good hints and traps of using this information.

- Ignore most sales as insiders sell the stocks for different reasons such as diversification, buying a mansion, divorce settlement, etc.
- Only consider sales if insiders are dumping most of the owned stocks. In this case, you want to short the stock.
- Consider the net purchases (= Total Purchases – Total Sales).
- Only consider purchases close to the market prices.
- Ignore all options.
- True insiders are officers such as CEO and CFO.
- 'Cluster purchases' is a better indicator.
- Consider market timing. When the market is going to plunge, all stocks most likely will go down.
- Consider basic fundamentals. If the fundamentals are bad, the stock most likely will not rise. There are exceptions such as approval of a new drug or unexpected profit.
- Consider technical analysis and charts.

This book guides you step-by-step to make the entire process profitable and easy to follow. First, it provides you with the best, free websites to obtain insiders' purchases and shows you how to separate real gems from garbage for maximum appreciation potential.

I have two performance summaries: one based on my stocks with insiders' purchases and one from a website. Both prove that following insiders' purchases is profitable.

This book started with Market Timing. When the market is going to plunge, most stocks including those with heavy insiders' purchases will lose value. Hence, do not buy any stocks and sell most stocks when you receive the exit signal.

I have a simple chart to identify market plunges. It depends on the stock data, so it will not identify the peaks and the bottoms precisely, but it will spare you for further losses and will instruct you when to reenter the market. It worked for the last two market crashes. It will detect the next crash, and hopefully it will give us enough time to react as the last two.

The selected website identifies stocks with insiders' purchases. Ignore those purchases that do not meet our requirements. We should have identified a few stocks for further evaluation. I use fundamental metrics to ensure they are fundamentally sound. Many fundamental analyses are available free from many sites. Then look for intangibles and do a thorough qualitative analysis on each selected stock. There is no magic formula, but due diligence will pay off in the long run. This book does not promise overnight wealth.

Other topics include how to set order prices, stop loss, tax considerations and a trade plan (Section IV). When to sell a stock is important. Technical analysis is used sparingly but it could be very useful. In some cases, it shows the uptrend of the stock before insiders' purchases.

Periodically review your big losers and big gainers to see whether any lessons to be learned.

As in any strategy, you need to start with paper trading and then with limited positions. There are many pitfalls in following insider purchases. It is safer to buy stocks with good fundamentals and protect the losses with stops.

This book is intended for a retail investor and I am one myself. This book is not written by a journalist or a professional writer who may never make a buck in the stock market.

The strategies described here have been used in my book Best Stocks 2014, According to Me. From 12/16/13 (the publish date) to 3/4/14, the list of all 135 selected stocks beat SPY (a ETF simulating the S&P 500 index) by 103% and the list of 9 small cap stocks beat SPY by 500%. There are similar results from later books in this series.

How this book is organized

This book has 6 sections covering most areas in insider trading.

Most graphs and tables are in landscape orientation (recommended for small screens) for both paperback and e-readers. Some graphs may not be displayed adequately on a small screen of an e-reader. E-readers may be available in the current version of Windows, so you can read e-books on the larger screen of your PC. For better orientation, just flip the e-readers 90 degrees. Some reader lets you select a table or a graph to display it to fit the screen.

A link is usually included for the most screens. Copy it to your browser to display the graphs on your PC if desirable. Instructions on how to produce some graphs are provided as you should try them out. One example is how to produce a chart on detecting market crashes.

The **font size** (Ctrl Minus for browser implementation of e-readers) and line spacing of most e-book formats can be adjusted. The unknown, special character is the "smiling face" that the current Kindle does not convert correctly as of this writing.

There are clickable links to web articles. Most of them are from my own websites and public websites such as Wikipedia. Some public links may not be available in the future as they are not under my control and my book offerings may change.

These links extend the usefulness of this book by making available specific topics that may not be interesting to every reader. It also provides articles (most are not written by me) for more in-depth analyzes.

Fidelity Video provides video clips to explain some basic terms and it may require Fidelity customers to sign on in order to view them. Check the trial offer from Fidelity. YouTube offers similar video lessons.

The current version provides most of the links the paperback readers can enter into your browser. Get the same information by entering a search in Wikipedia such as Dogs of Dow.

Investopedia is another source beside Wikipedia.
http://www.investopedia.com/

'Afterthoughts' includes my additional comments and ideas of minor importance.

There are fillers with tips, refreshing pictures (taken by me) and jokes (most original) to fill up the empty space of the printed book. Fillers, links and afterthoughts may disrupt the flow of reading this book. However, no readers so far ask me to take them out even in the digitized version of this book. Many page breaks have been eliminated to improve the flow of the book.

For convenience, this book uses SPY, an Exchange Traded Fund (ETF) simulating the S&P 500, as the benchmark for the market.

Annualized returns (Return * 365 / (Days between)) are used where appropriate for more meaningful comparison. To illustrate, I have a 10% return in 6 months, a 10% in a year and a 10% in 2 years. It is more meaningful to use annualized returns of 20%, 10% and 5% respectively in this example.

Usually I do not include the dividend, so you can add an estimated 1.5% to the annualized return. In addition, compound interest is not used for easier calculation, so the actual return could be even better. Many of my tests are not detailed in this book but their summaries are. It reduces the size of this book that is already huge.

About the author

I graduated from Cal. State University at San Jose in Industrial Engineering and University of Mass. in Amherst with a MS in Industrial Engineering. My last job was in IT. I have been an investor for over 30 years.

Dedication
To all retail investors and future retail investors including my grandchildren. I sincerely hope this book will build bridges with fellow investors with different backgrounds.

Acknowledgement
Thanks to all the free sites that make this book useful.

Important notices
© 2013-22 Tony Pow. Email ID: pow_tony@yahoo.com.

Version	Paperback	Kindle
1.0	01/15	01/15
3.1	06/20	06/20
3.3	04/22	04/22

Printed version of ISBN-13: 978-1494330019 or ISBN-10: 1494330016
No part of this book can be reproduced in any form without the written approval of the author with the following exception.

Disclaimer

Do not gamble with money that you cannot afford to lose. Past performance is a guideline and is not necessarily indicative of future results. All information is believed to be accurate, but there is not a guarantee. All the strategies including charts to detect market plunges described have no guarantee that they will make money and they may lose money. Do not trade without doing due diligence and be warned that most data may be obsolete. All my articles and the associated data are for informational and illustration purposes only. I'm not a professional investment counselor, a tax professional or any other field. Seek one before you make any investment decisions. Remember to consult with a registered financial adviser before making any investment decisions. The above mentioned also applies for all other advice such as on accounting, taxes, health and any topic mentioned in this book. Tax laws change all the time, so talk to your tax advisors before taking any action. Some articles may offend some one or some organization unintentionally. If I did, I'm sorry about that. I am politically and religiously neutral. I have provided my best efforts to ensure the accuracy of my articles. Data also from different sources was believed to be accurate. However, there is no guarantee that they are accurate and suitable for the current market conditions and /or your individual situations. The values of some parameters such as RSI(14) are arbitrarily set by me. I have made a lot of predictions that may not materialize. My publisher and I are not liable for any damages in using this book or its contents.

How the rate of return is calculated

They are for education purposes only, and do not make your investing decisions based on them. I usually use annualized for better comparisons; 4% in a month is more than 5% in a year for example. For short-term strategies including momentum, shorting and year-end strategy, I use the returns for a month, and sometimes including returns for 2 months for comparison. Annualized returns are usually used for long-term strategies. The holding periods may have a few days off due to holidays and weekends. For simplicity, most of my returns do not include commissions, exchange fees, order spread and dividends. Most numbers have been rounded up for better readability. The return = profit / investment. I and my publisher are not liable for any error. I use SPY and sometimes RSP as a yardstick; RSP and SPY have the same S&P 500 stocks, but the stocks are weighed evenly in RSP. However, many readers do not know RSP.

1   Define Insider Trading

Investopedia defines it as:

"Insider trading can be illegal or legal depending on when the insider makes the trade: it is illegal when the material information is still nonpublic-- trading while having special knowledge is unfair to other investors who don't have access to such knowledge. Illegal insider trading therefore includes tipping others when you have any sort of nonpublic information. Directors are not the only ones who have the potential to be convicted of insider trading. People such as brokers and even family members can be guilty.

Insider trading is legal once the material information has been made public, at which time the insider has no direct advantage over other investors. The SEC, however, still requires all insiders to report all their transactions. So, as insiders have an insight into the workings of their company, it may be wise for an investor to look at these reports to see how insiders are legally trading their stock."

If you need more information, click this link from Wikipedia.
http://en.wikipedia.org/wiki/Insider_trading

My additions to conventional insider trading

Hopefully my additions improve the performance of this strategy that has already been proven to work most of the time.

- I add market timing to Insider Trading. You need to sell most stocks except contra ETFs before or during a market plunge and buy them back as indicated by the chart; I provide a simple marketing technique without charts.

- Diversify your portfolio. Keep 10 stocks for a portfolio less than a million. Ensure that there are not more than 3 stocks in the same sector. Keep 20 stocks for a portfolio over a million. Too many stocks would require more of your time that would be better spent in evaluating individual stocks. However, keeping too few stocks would impact your portfolio when one stock has a big loss.

It is just a recommendation. Vary your holding size and holding period according to your time, your portfolio size and your knowledge in investing.

- Stick with stocks over $2, average daily volume over 12,000 shares (8,000 for stock prices over $20) and market cap over 200 million.

   Most big winners usually are in the price range between the $2 and $15 price and market cap between 200 million to 800 million. They represent the stocks that institutional investors are ignoring due to their restrictions. This is just a general guideline and there are always exceptions. Change them according to your requirements.

   I prefer to skip stocks from most emerging countries, especially the smaller companies, as I do not trust their financial statements.

- Ignore the subscription services or books claiming they are making over 30% consistently. Some even have examples of making 5,000%. Most likely they tell you their winners but not their losers. It is easy to pick up winners that fit their strategies, but they do not tell you the real performance.

   Check whether their portfolio uses cash, as it cannot be manipulated such as using the best prices of the day to trade. I bet that most portfolios consistently making over 30% are not real. Alternatively, they have 10 portfolios, and they only show you the one that makes a good profit.

   When they back test their strategies, they cheat their performances with survivor bias (i.e. those bankrupt stocks are not in the historical database). If their returns are that great, do you think they will share their secrets with you?

   Many made great fortune, but lost it all on a bad bet. So, the turtle investors who make small profits consistently fare far better than making millions in a year and losing it all in the next year. Market timing and diversifying our portfolio are our tools and they will beat the market in the long run.

2 Outline on how to start

1. First determine your risk tolerance, how much time you have for investing, your knowledge in investing and your portfolio size. When the market is risky, do not buy any stock.

2. Find stocks with heavy insider purchases.

3. Ensure the screened stocks are fundamentally sound.

4. Sell the stock when it fulfills your objective or the market is plunging.

5. Paper trade your strategy.

6. When it is thoroughly tested out and the result is good, use real money slowly and gradually. Monitor your performance.

While most of my predictions are materialized, some are not. Learn from the arguments for the predictions, not the predictions themselves. When the predictions are based on educated guesses, more of them will be materialized in the long run. I do not use predictions after-the-fact as many do.

Example of a filler (initially for the printed books)

Buy Low and Sell High

The market has a crash about every 4 years. As of 2015, this is overdue and it may not be it. Crisis also means opportunity in Chinese. A retail investor should be emotionally detached in making investment decisions. Buy low and sell high is always the best strategy I can think of.

Contents

Why you invest 2
Why you trust me 3
My amazing returns 4
Introduction 10
    Disclaimer 14
    How the rate of return is calculated 14
    1   Define Insider Trading 15
    2   Outline on how to start 17
    3   How to profit 21
        Canary warning? 22
    4   My trades based on insider purchase trading 24
Section I: Insider Purchases: Screening 24
    1   Screen the Insiders' purchase. 25
        Using Finviz.com 28
    2   Other Considerations 29
Section: Pick stocks for appreciation 31
    1   *Fundamental metrics* 32
        Testing key metrics 41
    2   Finviz's parameters 45
        Your broker's website 52
        Fidelity stock research 52
        Other sources 53
        Gurus 54
        Quick and dirty 54
        5-minute stock evaluation 55
    3   Intangibles 56
    4   Qualitative analysis 60
    5   Sectors to be cautious with 64

6	A scoring system	67
7	Examples of overpriced stocks	72
8	Avoid bankrupting companies	73
9	Technical analysis (TA)	75
10	More on technical analysis	77
11	An example on technical analysis	79
	Easy TA without charts	82
	Bollinger Bands	82
	MACD	84
12	Monitor your traded stocks	85

Section III: Other strategies 86

1	Refined Dogs of Dow	86
2	Tom's conservative strategy	90
3	The best strategy	92
	The second best strategy	95
	The third best strategy	96

Section IV: Trading stocks 97

1	Order prices	97
2	Stop loss & flash crash	101
3	Short selling	104
4	Covered calls	109
5	Diversification	112
6	*When to sell a stock*	115
7	Selling a winner	120
8	Tax avoidance	122
9	Trade plan	125

Section V: Market timing 130

1	The power of market timing	131
2	Market cycle	135
3	Calendar Timing	140

	Summary	142
4	Politics and investing	144
5	Market timing example	149
	Management summary	149

Review 154
Before and after insider trading 159
Bonus: Simple Techniques 160
    How to start 160
    1   Simplest market timing 161
    2   Quick analysis of ETFs 164
    An example 167
    3   Rotate four ETFs 168
    4   Simplest ways to evaluate stocks 170
    5   Simplest technical analysis 174
    6   The best strategy 175
    7   Don'ts for beginners 175
    8   Summary 176
    Bonus: Investing for 'lazy' folks 177
    Bonus: Sample portfolio 179
Epilogue 181
Appendix 1 – All my books 182
    Best stocks to buy for 2022 182
    Sector Rotation: 21 Strategies 183
    Investing Strategies: Build, Monitor and Execute 183
    Shorting Stocks and ETFs 184
Appendix 2 – Art of Investing 185
    Your choice for your next book 188
Appendix 3 - Our window to the investing world 189
Appendix 4 - ETFs / Mutual Funds 190

3   How to profit

My own monitor

The following is one of my performance monitors from the stocks I bought for over a period of 6 months.

All 372 stocks	77 stocks with Insiders' Purchases	Beat all stocks by
21%	28%	33%

This test was performed on 9/7/2013. They were the actual stocks I screened from the screens that had been proven. Insider Purchase is one of the fundamental metrics I monitored. The total number of stocks is 372 and 77 are identified as having heavy insider purchases. Stocks are bought in different periods. The returns are not annualized and dividends are not included. Most stocks have a holding period longer than 6 months.

If I started to collect data again, I would have used annualized returns and compared the returns to the market.

The test results are consistent with my previous tests. Beating all stocks by 33% is quite convincing. I conclude following insiders' purchases work most of the time at least in this period.

I conducted another test using the website OpenInsider on 11/2013. It listed all the insiders' purchases for more than a year. Selected insider purchases about 1 year ago by the Officer (CEO and CFO) only. I skipped the purchases that do not meet the requirements.

The annualized return is 50%. I only had about 50 stocks and it is not enough evidence to draw a conclusion. Even with 40% return, the strategy proves itself again.

My suggestion

Evaluate the purchased stocks again in 6 months. Sell the ones whose fundamental metrics have deteriorated or the price targets have been met.

Consider market timing. Sell most stocks when the chart indicates that the market is plunging.

Consider the total return. If you can wait for a month or so for less taxes on long-term capital gain, do so. If you expect that your stock does not appreciate a lot in the next few months, consider covered calls (similar to collecting rent with the renter's option to buy the housing unit at a specific price and time).

An example

Sometimes all experts are wrong on a stock except the insiders. Today (2/5/2015), GLUU is up by 23% with a good earnings report. It is 31% up since I bought it on 1/28/15, just 8 days ago. The annualized return must be astronomical.

I bought it based on the **favorable Insiders' Purchases** and confirmed by a good earnings rating (second best) from Zacks. Pow EY was 7% (passed), my short-term score 4 (failed), my long-term score 16 (just passed) and Pow Score 2 (just passed). The quarter-to-quarter profits and sales were spectacular at 200%.

The experts were wrong when I evaluated the stock: Safety Margin ridiculously negative, Blue Chip Growth C, Shorter 17%, Fidelity Equity Summary Score 4 (1 to 10 with 10 the best), ROE 3%, SMA %(10, 20 and 200 days) all negative (not good), IBD composite grade 33 (far below the average) and its SMD grade D.

Canary warning?
When I was working on my new book "Best stocks to buy for 2021" on Dec. 10, 2020, I found something really strange. I have never rejected so many stocks that have Fidelity's Equity Summary Score higher than 9. I rejected them as there was a lot of dumping from the insiders. Insiders know their companies better than most of us. Is it the canary telling us the market is overvalued?

Initially the following stocks have been screened by my value screens. Buy any one of the following stocks, **only** if you have good reason(s).

How can HEAR score a perfect 10 while the Insiders' Transaction is -75% (to me -2% is normal). The analysts must be wrong this time, or they believe the market will continuously make new heights.

Symbol	Fidelity Score	Insider Purchase	Return[1]	Annualized
BCC	9.9	-24%	46%	126%
GPI	10.0	-17%	35%	95%
HEAR	10.0	-75%	43%	118%
HVT	9.5	-37%	53%	144%
HZO	9.5	-27%	75%	204%
Average				84%
SPY				30%
Beat SPY[2]				177%

[1] From Dec. 20, 2020 to July 1, 2021. Fees, commissions and dividends are not included.

[2] = (Average − SPY) /SPY. SPY represents the market to many of us. This concludes the Insiders are wrong in this case.

4   My trades based on insider purchase trading

Insiders' Purchases should be very positive for the appreciation of the stock. Who knows better than the insiders, the ones who run the business daily? However, I prefer sound fundamentals too. I use Finviz.com's screener on stocks that have "very positive insider transactions".

The following are one test. The end date is 12/15. POZN has a wild swing.

Stock	Buy Date	Return	Annualized
POZN	05/08/15	-10%	-21%
LAKE	07/16/15	15%	55%
ABTL	07/16/15	21%	78%

Section I: Insider Purchases: Screening

There are many sites to screen Insider Purchases. I select the ones that should give us the best result and are free.

Screening is only the first step. Need to filter the good ones from the bad ones.

In addition to the one from OpenInsider.com (could be the best and described next), here are some other sites:

InsiderTrading.com
http://insidertrading.org/
Fizviz.com provides many useful functions besides insider trading.
InsiderCow.com
http://www.insidercow.com/
InsiderMonkey.com
http://www.insidermonkey.com/

Page 25

1 Screen the Insiders' purchase.

Bring up OpenInsider.com
(http://www.openinsider.com/)

SEC Form 4						
Filing Date	Trade Date	Sym	Company	Insider		Shares	Transaction	Value
Nov 19 02:32pm	Nov 18 2013	OCN	Ocwen Financial Corp	Hayes Timothy M	EVP, Gen. Counsel, Secretary	1,000	Purchase at $52.44	$52,440
Nov 19 02:14pm	Nov 15 2013	ONTX	Onconova Therapeutics, Inc.	Reddy E Premkumar	Director	5,000	Purchase at $12.10	$60,500
Nov 19 01:37pm	Nov 19 2013	MVIS	Microvision Inc	Tokman Alexander Y	President, CEO	20,000	Purchase at $1.35	$27,000
Nov 19 01:28pm	Nov 18 2013	CEN	Center Coast Mlp & Infrastructure Fund	Curran Michael F	Director	5,000	Purchase at $19.00	$95,000
Nov 19 01:15pm	Nov 15 2013	PDII	Pdi Inc	Belle Gerald P	Director	20,400	Purchase at $5.21	$106,266
Nov 19 12:54pm	Nov 15 2013	MCBF	Monarch Community Bancorp Inc	Ross Stephen Millard	Director	12,500	Purchase at $2.00	$25,000
Nov 19 12:47pm	Nov 15 2013	MCBF	Monarch Community Bancorp Inc	Mitchell Martin L	Director	100,000	Purchase at $2.00	$200,000
Nov 19 12:35pm	Nov 15 2013	MCBF	Monarch Community Bancorp Inc	Loomis Karl F	Director	125,000	Purchase at $2.00	$250,000
Nov 19 12:11pm	Nov 19 2013	MM	Millennial Media Inc	Palmieri Paul J	President, CEO	10,000	Purchase at $5.92	$59,220
Nov 19 11:42am	Nov 15 2013	AF	Astoria Financial Corp	Chrin John R	Director	1,656	Purchase at $22.17	$36,768

Source: OpenInsider
The following is for illustration purposes only. This screen is displayed on 11/19/2013.

If your screen is too small, bring up your PC's browser, and type:

http://ebmyth.blogspot.com/2013/12/insider-screen-for-profit-from-insider.html

Here is an illustration looking for candidates.

- Select the Officers only. Including the Director is the second choice.
- Ignore the transactions that have values less than $100,000. We only have PDII and MCBF. You should not have the same stocks on a different date. Select the stocks that have purchase values more than $100,000.
- Next bring up Finviz.com in your browser. Enter PDII and scroll all the way down to find the net purchase (= purchase amount − sold amount). For example, if the insiders bought $100,000 worth of stock and they sold $100,000 of your stock, it would not be considered as a purchase. There was no insider sell for PDII, so it is fine.
- Was the stock purchased close to the market price? From Finviz.com again, the purchase price was $5.25 and the current price is $5.29. So it looks good.

Summary of selected criteria

The displayed screen does not have all the selection criteria as below.

- Select Officer only.
- Filing Date and Trade Date within the last 7 days.
- Transactions: Purchase only.
- Sorted by Value. Omit transactions less than $100,000 (adjust to the value you're comfortable with).

Skip the stocks if they are one of the following (change them to your own requirements).

- The purchase price is not close to the market price.
- Penny stocks (less than $2) or market cap less than 50 million. It is too risky to me, but it is your call.
- Stock daily volume less than 8,000 shares (I prefer 10,000).
- Poor fundamentals. If you do not have time to do a thorough analysis, use Fidelity's Equity Summary Score. GuruFocus.com (fee) has a nice evaluation with warning signs.
- If they are not listed in one of the three major exchanges.

My steps

Be flexible and use the tools you have.

1. Select the stocks with heavy insider trading. OpenInsider.com provides many features. Select Officers, Purchase Only, and Last 7 Trade Days and Last 7 File Days. Sorted by Trade Value.

   As an alternative, Finviz's screener is easy to find these stocks.

2. Use Finviz.com. Understand the company and their fundamentals.

   If the stock cannot be found, most likely it is not traded here. Skip these companies and also the companies with small market caps and average daily volumes.

   Check the insider trade prices. If the trade prices are too low from the market prices, skip these stocks.

   Understand the company such as the country, the sector and general financial shape. I would skip most foreign countries especially from emerging countries and small companies as I do not trust their financial information.

   For safety, I would examine the fundamentals of the screened stocks.

   Skip the companies that have more than 5% appreciation in the last 5 days. We may have missed this boat, but there are many other boats.

3. Use OpenInsider.com again to list the 90 days transactions (all) for the stock. If the CEO sells 1,000 shares and buys back 1,000 shares, there is no insider purchase.

#Filler: My daughter's wedding

How to have a wedding banquet that the entire town will talk about and at the least cost? It is at the Burger King where they treat you like a king. All the fries are super-sized and the drinks are bottomless. The king's crown and the most popular party favor, are included. Of course, my daughter flatly refused.

Using Finviz.com

Bring up Finviz.com from your browser and select Screener. There are three groups of filter criteria. Sort the stocks using Insider Transaction in descending order.

Suggested Common Criteria:

Criteria	Value
Description	
Relative Volume	Over 2
Country	USA
Technical	
20-Day Simple Moving Avg.	Price 10% above
Volatility	Week – Over 3%
Fundamental	
Insider Transactions	Very Positive (>20%)
The next 2 are optional	
Institutional Ownership	Over 10%
Forward P/E	Under 35

You may want to vary the parameters to suit your requirements.

For value investors, select Forward P/E less than 20 and earning is positive and market cap is larger (over 500 M for example).

In my example, I find 15 stocks for that time. I narrow them to 2. First, I skip all stocks that already have more than 10% rise. They may have risen too high already. Select profitable stocks with forward P/E less than 25. "Debt/Equity" is less than .5 (50%). Then, "ROI" is higher than 25%. Stop when you have reached the optimal number of stocks (2 for me in this example). If you find too many stocks, tighten the criteria and vice versa. Save the criteria and the selected stocks in a portfolio for paper trading.

When the stock looks attractive, enter it into OpenInsider.com to ensure the purchases are meaningful. Both Institution transaction and Insider transaction from Finviz.com are important.

2 Other Considerations

Do not bet the entire farm on any trade

We have a better chance to make money, but it is no guarantee as in everything else in life. To reduce the loss, we should evaluate the stock completely. Sometimes we still lose due to the reasons below.

- The insiders trick us to buy their company's stock.
- The stock has been manipulated.
- Even insiders make mistakes.
- The market is not rational.
- It takes the market longer to realize the potential value of the stock. In this case, hold on to the stock if it is fundamentally sound.
- The market plunges.
- Some unforeseeable event(s) happen.

Considerations

- Officers predict the stock prices better. OpenInsider.com gives us a choice on the classification of the purchasers. In addition, **ignore options exercised by the officers**.

- Consider the total value amount of the insiders' purchases. The value should be tied to the market cap. A small purchase for a small company is more significant than the same amount for a company with a market cap of several billions.

- **Compare the value to the purchase's annual salary.** If he or she bets more than his or her salary, the action is more significant.

- Any purchase by more than one officer is a good sign.

- Officers made small buys and then sold a big chunk several months later. It is called 'pump and sell'. We cannot detect it as the sell is in the future. That's why we have to evaluate the fundamentals of the company and do not bet the entire farm on a single purchase.

- Officers may make a purchase for the following reasons to jack up the price. These purchases should be ignored.
    - Most have a lot of stocks and options, so it is to their benefit to have their stock price stay high. It also explains why officers prefer stock buyback.

    - Prevent the company stock price to fall below a certain level that it would be delisted or would prevent analysts and fund managers from researching the stock.

- Watch out when the execution date (same as the trade date) and the announcement date. If it is too far apart, then it would not be a good indicator.

- Watch out for today's date. If they're too far away from the trade date, it may not be meaningful.

- Compare the number of shares purchased to the total number of shares the insider already has. If it is a very small percentage, the insider could use it to boost confidence and hence the stock price.

- Watch out for purchases after a disaster such as a bad earnings announcement. Executives are humans and they could believe wrongly that they have found the bottom value and/or they're overconfident in their own company.

- A good executive may not be a good trader and most cannot predict when the market plunges. That's why we have to watch out for market plunges.

- Most executives understand their companies and the sector their company is in. However, when they have too much confidence and love in their company, they could be biased and lose their reasoning. To illustrate that, everyone knew PCs would take over mini computers except the CEOs of the mini computer companies such as DEC and Wang. They're geniuses, but their minds had been covered by their egos, love, optimism, bias and overconfidence.

Section: Pick stocks for appreciation

After the market is not risky (Section I) and we have picked up stocks (Section II), we still need to evaluate the stocks. Most stocks with bad fundamentals will not appreciate. However there are examples on turnaround situations (some call them catalysts) such as:

- A new drug has positive test result.
- A new product.
- A new discovery or breakthrough.
- Being acquired.
- Being settled with a major lawsuit.

Screen stocks first and then analyze the screened stocks one by one.

The most updated information is from the Earning Conference Call (easier to obtain it from SeekingAlpha), Q10 report and from the company's website. Finviz.com seems to be more updated than most other sites besides the above.

When to sell a stock? I have three chapters at the end of this section. They are in the same topic but in different approaches / concepts.

The better analysis gives you better chance of success, but as everything in life there is no guarantee.

Myths on dividend stocks

- Dividend yield determines the value of a stock. Not true. Apple did not pay good dividend for a long while. Many financial stocks with great dividend yield bankrupted in 2008.

    How about borrow money to pay dividends?

- P/B is one of the 3 pillars (besides dividend yield and P/E). Not true as the book value does not contain intangibles that could worth a lot especially for established companies.

1   *Fundamental metrics*

ROE

Return of equity (ROE = Net Income / Equity) could be the most important financial indicator to determine how well the management is doing their job. However, in recent years, this metric has been overused and loses its prediction reliability.

The company's return on equity for at least the last five years would indicate how the stock price endures major financial downturns as well as upturns.

Comparing the ROE to the average ROE for the sector is a good indicator on how well the company is managed compared to its peers. Some sectors including utilities have low average ROEs.

Market Cap (Capitalization)
Market Cap = Total no. of outstanding shares * share price

I recommend the beginners buy U.S. stocks with a market cap greater than 800 M (million). Here are the current conventions (everyone's convention is different) and they should be adjusted to inflation.

Class	Market Cap (million)
Nano Cap	< $50M
Micro Cap	$50M to $250M
Small Cap	$250M to $1B (billion)
Mid Cap	$1B to $10B
Large Cap (Blue Chip)	$10B to $50B
Mega Cap	>50B

The higher the cap is, usually the less risky the stock would be. Nano Cap and Micro Cap are reserved for speculators or owners of the companies. Small Cap and Mid Cap are for knowledgeable investors as most institutional investors would skip these stocks in these caps especially Small Cap. Large Cap, Mega Cap and some Mid Cap are the stocks traded by institutional investors. They are thoroughly researched continuously.

My metrics

My current favorites are Forward P/E, PEG, Fidelity's Equity Summary Score, Short % of outstanding shares, Free Cash Flow, ROE and Debt Load / Equity.

In addition, I use many summarized metrics from different sources. For example, one of my subscription services gives me a composite rank for fundamentals and another one for momentum. To illustrate, click here for Blue Chip Growth which is no longer free for stock analysis. Enter IBM as the stock symbol. As of 2/2013, it gives C for a Total Grade, D for Quantity Grade and B for Fundamental Grade. The Total Grade is usually a composite grade of other grades.

Use the metrics to screen through the stocks to reduce the number of stocks for further consideration.

Mid, high and low values of common metrics

Metric	Mid Range	Low Range	High Range
P/E (last 12 months)	< 10	>40	< 4
Price / Cash Flow	< 12	>30	< 4
Price / Sales	< 2.5	>3	< .2
Price / Book	< 2.0	>4	< .2
PEG	< 1.5	>2	< .2

High Range means good values (although in this table it means low numbers), but sometimes it is too good to be true. Low Range means bad values. To illustrate, many internet stocks in 2000 had P/E over 40 (bad) while a neglected bargain stock has a P/E of 3 (supposed to be good). A bargain could also mean they could have some hidden problems. In reality, I prefer the Mid Range. Using P/E to illustrate, it should be between 4 and 10. Adjust the range according to your personal tolerance and the current market conditions. If the market trend is up, you may want to relax the range to 5 to 12 for example otherwise you cannot find too many stocks for further evaluation.

These values are my selections based on data for about 10 years. They are used for predicting the performance of a stock in a year; review the ranges every 6 months in the current market.

The metrics with the high-range and mid-range values offer better predictions for the stock price appreciation. From the above table, the stocks with the low-range values have a better chance than other stocks to lose money in a year or so. Some favorable numbers could be high values instead of low values such as ROE.

However, the range values could change. When the market favors momentum or you do not keep stocks for less than a month or so, the momentum metrics including PEG and price growth could be better predictors. We need to check to see whether the current market favors which metrics: Value or Growth – some websites and subscription services identify the current favorite. In addition, the performance of each metric should be evaluated every 3 to 6 months. In addition, new range values need to be adjusted with the above table.

Fundamental metrics take a longer time (about 6-12 months vs. 1 month for momentum metrics) for the performance to materialize. The metrics in the above table besides PEG are all fundamental metrics. Except for financial stocks, P/B is always worthless.

Examples of searching with high range values

Stocks with low-range values for most metrics (such as 40 in P/E in the above table) could be risky. Hence, select the stocks with the mid-range value (e.g., 10 for P/E). Avoid the low-range values indicated by the metrics.

Here is one example of selecting stocks with high range values of P/E and P/B. Most likely, you will not find too many stocks with these criteria.

```
E > 0     and
P/E < 4 and
P/B < .2
```

E is earning per share and we need the company to be profitable.

High range values could indicate something is wrong with the company, e.g., a lawsuit pending. I would consider a P/E of less than 4 is suspicious. However, very small companies are often neglected by the market, so they could be solid companies. Don't forget to do your due diligence and spend more time in thoroughly evaluating the stock and its industry.

The stocks with the low-range values have a greater chance of losing money in the next year or so. That is proven statistically as a group despite some exceptions. AMZN[2] is not a valued stock by its high P/E or its high P/B. However, if the company is investing for the future by building infrastructure and capturing the market share, you may ignore these unfavorable metrics. Personally, I prefer fundamentally sound companies today.

Note. P/B is not a good metric for established companies and / or companies with a lot of research such as IBM. Many metric formulae are outdated due to ignoring intellectual properties, patents and market appeals such as brand names.

Example of a search for mid-range values
E > 0 and
P/E < 10 and
P/E > 4

In this case, you only include companies with positive earnings and P/Es within the range from 4 to 10 exclusively. You should find many companies with the mid-range values of P/Es.

Add other filters such as minimum price, market cap and average volume. If you do not find too many stocks, relax your criteria (start with mid-range values in the table), and vice versa to limit the number of stocks. If you usually find stocks with a screen but not today, it usually means that the market is overvalued and that you cannot find many bargain stocks.

Again, it is the first step to narrow down the number of stocks to be analyzed. Your metrics will not cover stocks with special situations. For example, IBM always has had a high Price/Book value for as long as I can remember and therefore it does not mean it should be excluded.

The searches based on fundamental metrics help us to narrow stocks for further evaluation. Occasionally I abandon the scoring system for some stocks under special conditions.

Compare a company's metrics to its sector's averages
This could be the most powerful comparison: Compare Apples to Apples.

You may want to compare the metrics of a company to the averages of that sector. The average of supermarket's P/S is extremely low and hence it has no meaning to compare a supermarket's P/S to most other sectors. Some sectors like utilities need high debt to run a utility company.

However, when the average P/E or other metric of a sector is suddenly lower than its historical average, it could mean that sector is out-of-favor and/or the sector is having a better value.

This following table compares Apple to its sector and a retail sector on a specific date for illustration. All the metrics will change.

Metric	Apple	Computer	Retail
P/E	11	19	24
(5-year average)	16	17	15
PEG	.6	N/A	1.4
Price /Cash Flow	9.4	8.1	9.2
Price /Book	3.3	3.0	3.6
EPS Growth	-6%	-42%	2.6%
(last 5 years)	62%	45%	11%
Operating Margin	20%	15%	8%
ROE	30%	14%	19%
Debt / Equity	2%	7%	88%
Inventory Turnover	76%	53%	4.55x

From the above table, some metrics only make sense for an industrial sector (Computer for Apple). In this case, you may want to compare AAPL to Computer, and not to Retail.

"Debt / Equity" indicates that the retail sector needs to borrow more than the computer sector for example. Of course, retail stores have high Inventory Turnover.

Top-down approach

First, compare whether the market is risky. Second, select the best sector; there are many sites including Finviz.com to select the best sector. Then compare the fundamental metrics of the major stocks within that sector.

Some metrics do not apply

Using financial institutions as an example, usually P/B is more useful than P/CF. However, the quality of a loan (not a metric here) is more important than all metrics as we found out in 2007. P/S is more important for retails. However, the expected P/E is most important for most other sectors.

When you believe a sector is the currently best (a criterion available in many screeners), select the best stocks in this sector.

Compare metrics to its five-year average

If the company's five-year average of P/E (available from Fidelity and many other sites) is 20 and today it is 10. It is 100% under-valued by this standard. Also, you may want to try other metrics such as debt/equity and compare it to the five-year average.

Growth Metrics

The growth metrics are growth rates of the stock price, sales, earnings, etc. They are useful for growth investors.

Even for value investors, the earnings growth rate is very important, as most stocks with substantial gains have increased their earnings growth first. If the earnings has grown but the price remains the same (i.e., PEG), then the potential for price appreciation will be higher and most likely it will return to the historical average P/E.

Momentum Metrics

Momentum metrics is part of growth. The rates of increase of the stock price, the volume... are the major metrics. Earnings revision is another one especially in earnings announcement seasons (usually 4 times a year).

Fidelity and many subscription services provide a composite rank with name Timely or similar name. The following could be part of this Timely score: SMA-50, Q-Q sales increase and recent price appreciation. In my momentum portfolio, I use these metrics and ignore all the other metrics as my average holding period is less than 30 days for momentum strategies.

Insiders' buying

Insiders sell their stocks for many reasons. When insiders buy a lot of their companies' stocks at market prices, take notice. Insiders know better than anyone about the health of their companies and their industries.

Select Insiders' purchases from one of the available sites such as Finviz.com. Ignore the option exercises. I prefer the high ratios of Net Total Purchase Value / Market Cap and the purchases by more than one insider. Be careful that the insiders purchase the stocks after selling a similar amount of stock in a brief time span.

OpenInsider is a good site for this info.
InsiderSights is a good one too with more capable tools that would take more time to learn.

Where to get the metrics
You can get this information from the website with no or low cost such as Finviz.com, your broker's site, AAII (very low cost) and Fidelity.

The following subscriptions are at a little higher cost but they are still less than $1,000 per year: Value Line, IBD, Zacks, VectorVest and Stock Screen 123. Many data from different vendors are duplicated such as P/E. You will save time by concentrating on one or two sources.

Many vendors provide a composite metric such as a value metric to cover P/E, debt... and a timing metric to cover Technical Analysis indicators, PEG, price appreciation rate...

Short % is a useful metric available in Finviz.com. For Fidelity customers, you can click on Research and then Stock. Enter the stock name, and then click on Detailed. I find Fidelity's Analysts' Opinions quite useful.

Finviz.com provides a lot of useful information free of charge. It also provides a screen function. The 'Help' button describes Finviz's functions and all the metrics monitored.

Other sources are: Insider Cow, NASDAQ Guru Analysis ...

Monitor the recent performance of the metrics
The predictability of most metrics has proven not to perform consistently as many investors and fund managers found out. My theory is that the

specific metric works better in some market conditions than others. To test which ones work better currently, check their performance in the last three months and use those that perform well. This is what my scoring system in the book Scoring Stocks is based on.

Why some metrics fail sometimes

Most investors are using metrics to screen stocks, but few are successful consistently. Some investment companies have top analysts dedicated to projects looking for the right strategy. My guesses why they fail are:

1. Metrics need to be monitored to see its effectiveness on current market conditions.
2. Besides fundamental metrics, there are many intangibles.
3. When they have too many followers on the same metrics, they will not work such as ROE in the last several years.
4. Fundamentals need time (at least 6 months) to reflect the value of the stock. You're swimming against the tide as a fundamentalist. Trading momentum stocks using basic fundamentals will not work.
5. Watch out 'Garbage in and garbage out'. Some emerging countries do not have an organization similar to SEC to ensure the integrity of the financial statements of a company and some audit firms are being paid to cover their eyes. Even though there are frauds in some U.S. companies and with their auditors.
6. The metrics may be derived from obsolete financial statements. Check out the date. The most updated one could be available from the company's website.
7. Some companies borrow a lot of money to dress up the metrics such as P/E and ROE. They will look good short-term but not long-term. Ensure the debt/equity has not been increased recently for this purpose. I recall one utility spin-off had incredible fundamentals except the debt load. It is so high that all these fundamentals will deteriorate in the future due to servicing its high debts.

Footnote

[1] The stocks are classified into sector and then sectors are divided into industries (same as sub sectors). For example, oil is a sector and oil exploration and oil services are industries under the oil sector. For simplicity, I intermix the terms here as many sectors do not need further sub classifications for this discussion.

[2] AMZN is not a value stock by any standard. As of 1/1/2013, its P/E (from last 12 months) is 157 and P/B is 15. Both fall far into my low-range values. Its price rises from 256 from 1/1/13 to 270 today (1/22/13). Today its P/E is ridiculously over 3,000. The investors are betting AMZN's internet sales will take over the concrete stores and its investors do not care about profit but rather for market share. Does it sound familiar in the internet era? Its price momentum is indicated positively by any chart. It may be a good stock for traders, but it is too risky for a swing trader and a long-term investor like me (yes, I wear two hats). I do not short stocks in a rising market, but this could be an exception.

Afterthoughts

- The only recommendation from a very popular investment book I read is to select stocks by the return of equity (ROE). I will save you the time and money to read that book. I read the entire book in an hour at Barnes and Noble's and it saved me some money / time, not to mention cutting down trees for that book. Basically, it does not work today.
- DAL has an interesting Debt / Equity of over -1000% due to the negative equity. For a comparison, you may want to use Debt / ABS(Equity).
- Once in a while, I found the financial data was not consistent from different sources. Try to check out any discrepancy in the dates of the financial data of your sources. The financial statements from the company websites usually have the most updated data.
- Current Ratio = Current Asset / Current Liability. If it is below 1, then the company is having a tough time in meeting its current cash obligations.
- Dividend Yield is a valid metric for matured companies. I do not use it to evaluate growth companies or companies that need to plow back cash for research and development.

- If you use Finviz.com, you find three margins: profit, gross and operating. I prefer to use profit margin that is more useful for most companies. The other two may be relevant in some sectors.

  http://www.investopedia.com/terms/p/profitmargin.asp
  http://www.investopedia.com/terms/g/grossmargin.asp
  http://www.investopedia.com/terms/o/operatingmargin.asp

Use Wikipedia for more description.
- Enron had millions in profits but negative cash flows. Earnings can be manipulated but not the cash flows.

  Insiders' selling usually does not cause any alarm unless excessively. Most insiders sell most of the stocks they have before these companies go bankrupt. Just common sense!
- Why fundamentals are important. (http://seekingalpha.com/article/1612442-its-shorting-season)

  On the same day when this article was published, RVLT was up 10% due to increasing sales in the earnings conference. However, the company is still not profitable. It shows how tough shorting is even with good arguments. That's why do not expect every purchase is profitable. However, with the educated guesses, you should beat the market in the long run.
- Due to my ignorance, limited time or my short period of holding stocks, I have not used intrinsic value that often.

  Book value is different from intrinsic value. Book value is calculated by summing up the values of all pieces of a company such as a building and all equipment.

  Intrinsic value is the real value of a company. When two companies have the same book value and market cap, the company that generates more profit than the other one usually has a higher intrinsic value. When the intrinsic value is higher than the stock price, it is underpriced in theory.

  Links:
  Income statement: https://www.youtube.com/watch?v=ht-tzwyLPU
  The following link provides more info on intrinsic value.
  http://en.wikipedia.org/wiki/Intrinsic_value_%28finance%2

Testing key metrics

Here is a summary table on my findings in a recent test. It is based on a small amount data from 1-5-2007 to 1-7-2014 (about one market cycle). This is for illustrating how to test metrics and I am not responsible for any error in preparing the results.

Metric	P/E	PEG	P/S	P/FC	P/B
Criteria	<3	<1	<.06	<10	<2

I used P/E growth rate of P/E instead of PEG and it is 8%. My average P/S is about .07, substantially smaller than .8 from other tests. If you have a historical database, you can test it out the above metrics and other metrics with the criteria described below.

Common testing criteria
The following are my basic criteria.
- Market Cap > 50 M.
- Price > 1 to reduce survivorship bias.
- Avg. Volume > 10,000.
- 3 Major Exchanges.
- EPS > 0. Only select stocks with positive earnings.

I started from 2007 and ended in 2013. I tested from the beginning of the year (actually with several days later due to no data on Jan. 1) to the end of the year. Repeat it for the next year and average the returns of all the 7 years. I call it 'window' testing to avoid the distorted value when you have a big win or loss in the early year.

To illustrate, I tested the above criteria with P/E and sort P/E in ascending order from 1/5/2007 to 1/4/2008. The top 10 stocks have an average of 44%. Repeated the test for the next 7 years.

Result
Here is the partial result

Metric	P/E	PEG	P/S	SPY
Avg. Return	13%	8%	38%	6%
Beat SPY	124%	35%	538%	N/A

However, from my Market Timing book, I should be out of the stock market in second part of 2007 and the entire 2008. The next table is from 2009 to 2013 instead of from 2007 and resembles my actual trading better.

Metric	P/E	PEG	P/S	SPY
Avg. Return	35%	19%	125%	13%
Beat SPY	166%	45%	864%	N/A

The above metrics beat SPY by a larger percent in the 'good' years than the first table.

P/B and P/FC (Free Cash) are obtained info from other sources. I also had P/S Growth and it did not beat SPY. It is ignored. P/S turns out to be very important metric.

To illustrate such as the 3 in P/E, I selected the highest value of the P/E in the top 10 stocks for each year and averaged the values from 5 tests (from 2009).

Instead of holding the stocks for 1 year, I tried 2 years. The result is worse, so stick with holding the stocks for 1 year.

The next step is to find the best combination in more than one metric and their values, such as "P/S < .06" and "P/E < 3". If I do not find a lot of stocks, I would relax the criteria such as "P/S < .08 and "P/E < 4".

This is just a general guideline. Different sectors have different metrics. Super market has a very different P/S than high tech companies for example.

Technical indicators

Bring up Finviz.com from your browser and enter the symbol of the stock.

Ensure the stock's SMA200 is above 0% as we do not want to buy stock in a downward trend. SMA200% is Single Moving Average for the last 200 trade sessions. The percent indicates how far the stock price from its SMA.

In addition, the RSI(14) should be less than 75, which would indicate the stock is overbought.

My calculation on SPY compared to MSN is a little off for the following reasons: 1. Not starting on Jan. 1 and ending on Dec. 31 for my convenience, and 2. Dividends are not included. As long as I use the same dates for other tests, it is quite OK for comparing with my test results. For better total return estimate, add 2% for dividend to my SPY for the annualized rate and then the difference is about 1%.

	My SPY (Few days diff)	MSN (with dividend)	Difference
Avg. 3 years	13%	17%	3%
Avg. 5 years	6%	9%	3%

Summary table

Metric	Value	Indicates	Relaxed
Market: (use SPY)			
SMA350%	Above 0	Not plunging	Above 0
SMA350%	>9	Correction possible	>12
RSI(14)	>65	Correction possible	>70
Fundamentals:			
P/E	<4	Good	<8
PEG	<1	Good	<1.2
P/S	<.07 (or even # .8)	Good	<.8
Technical:			
SMA200%	>0	Up trend	>1
SMA200%	<10	Not peaking	<15
RSI(14)	<70	Not overbought	<75

Relaxed values are what I use.

2   Finviz's parameters

Most metrics are described in Finviz (via Help), Investopedia and/or Wikipedia and my chapters on P/E and fundamental metrics if available. We use the metrics for screening stocks and then evaluating the screened stocks.

The following are my personal comments and why I feel some metrics are more important than the others. Personally, I divide the metrics into fundamentals and technical, which are more important for long-term investors and short-term investors respectively.

Compare the ratios to the companies in the same sector (industry) and also its averages from the last few years (5 preferable) from many other websites such as Fidelity.

From your browser, enter Finviz.com. Enter a symbol (I used ABEO for discussion). A chart is displayed with the prices and volumes for the last eleven months. SMAs (Single Moving Average) are displayed sometimes with other technical indicators. Intraday, Daily and Weekly options are available for day traders, short-term traders and long-term traders respectively. I prefer Candle – Advanced for drawing charts.

Besides the chart and the metrics described next, it describes what the company does, analysts' recommendations (I prefer Fidelity's Equity Summary Score), insiders' trading and articles that are good for intangible and qualitative analysis. Many free websites such as Yahoo!Finance provide a list of articles about the company.

"Financial Highlights and Statements" are materials for more in-depth analysis and they were more important decades ago when most financial ratios had not been calculated for you. It is important for investors with good knowledge in financial accounting. The current version also includes the basic balance sheet, income statement and cash flow for the current (TTM) and the last two years. Click on the following YouTube links for more detail.

Balance: https://www.youtube.com/watch?v=DMv9JC_K37Y
Income: https://www.youtube.com/watch?v=0--AvwZabIQ
Cash flow: https://www.youtube.com/watch?v=hMBN6yTIDb0

A section on Insider Trading is also included. Do not be alarmed when insiders dump small quantities of the stocks. Buying large quantities (e.g., insider transaction more than 5%) at prices close to the market price could be favorable news.

The following metrics are roughly based on the flow of Finviz from top to bottom and left to right. I skip those metrics that I believe are not too important. You can also place your cursor on the metric to retrieve the description from Finviz or via Finviz's Help. Some metrics are left blank to indicate they are not applicable (for example, zero, negative or not available). For example, the Debt/Equity of YRCW in 1/2019 is blank (same as null) due to its negative Equity. From Yahoo!Finance at the time of writing, it has a total debt of 888M.

- **Index**. Most of us trade stocks in the three major exchanges in the USA. Stocks listed over-the-counter are too risky for most of us. Skip the stocks in local exchanges and foreign exchanges unless you are an expert on these stocks and/or have insightful (not illegal info from insiders) information. I screen the stocks and then ignore the stocks that are not in the Dow, NASDAQ and Amex. Other screeners may let you select a group of exchanges.
- **Market Cap** (MC). To me, stocks below 50M are risky even though they could be very profitable. Ensure the Avg. Volume is at least 10,000 shares and / or your order is less than 1% of the average volume. Some small stocks are controlled by the owners and have small volumes. You cannot trade these stocks easily.

    Float = Outstanding shares – Insider shares

    Usually, Float does not matter as they are typically the same. However, it does for small companies with large insider shares. Most of these owners do not want to sell their family businesses and hence they reduce the chance of being acquired entirely or partially for good prices. In this case, you may have to hold this kind of stock for a long time or you may have to sell it at a very unfavorable price.
- If **Forward P/E** (a.k.a. Expected P/E) is not provided, use the P/E which is based on the trailing last 12 months (TTM). Alternatively, calculate the E by using the E from P/E and multiplying it by its growth rate. It may not be seasonally adjusted. I prefer using Forward P/E as it

provides a better predictability power to me. Successful investing is usually a result of correct guessing the future earnings.

Finviz.com leaves the P/E blank (same as null) if the earnings are negative. In this case, I would check out Yahoo!Finance's EV / EBITDA, which also considers taxes, cash and interests. The blank condition also happens in some other metrics such as negative assets (very seldom).

Earnings Yield is equal to E/P. I call it 'True Earnings Yield' for EBITDA / EV. It is easier to understand. Compare Earnings Yield or True Yield to the annual dividend yield of a 10-year Treasury – with the low interest rate in 2021, skip this comparison for this year.

E/P is easier in screening and sorting the screened stocks. If you use P/E instead of E/P, you need to screen or sort stocks with a clause "P/E > 0".

When the P/E is less than 5, be careful and there may be a reason why it is so low. Many bankrupting companies have low P/Es at one time before their stock prices go to zero..

Compare the P/E or Forward P/E with the average P/E for the sector and its average P/E for the last 5 years that are available from Fidelity.com. Some sectors such as technology have high P/Es (25 for me). If the sector is cyclical, the earnings could be affected.

When the prospect of the company is good such as Tesla in 2020, ignore P/E. Investors are betting on the future. Do not short these rocket stocks.

- **Cash / share**. It is used to calculate Pow P/E and Pow EY when EV/EBITDA for the stock is not available. To illustrate, if the stock is $10 and it has $10 cash / share without debt (i.e., Debt/Equity = 0), most likely it is underpriced as you can get the whole company for nothing. You should find out why the price is so low. It could be the market ignoring the stock, or there is a serious event happening such as a major lawsuit. P/C is a better choice than Cash/Share; the lower the better.
- **Dividend %** is useful for income investors. The payout ratio should not be more than 30% except for matured companies. Most developing companies and tech companies plough back the profits into research and development, and hence they do not pay dividends.

- **Recs**. Select stocks with 1 or 2. Do not base your stock selection on this recommendation alone. There have been many bad recommendations that could cost you a fortune in losses. Use Fidelity's Equity Summary Score instead.
- **PEG** is a measure of the growth of P/E and hence a growth metric (the other ones are Sales Growth Q-Q and Earnings Growth Q-Q). It is similar to P/E, but it takes the expected earnings growth rate into account. The lower value is better as long as earnings is positive. If earnings is negative, then the reverse is true. It is a defect in using P/E and PEG and that's why I recommend EY (Earnings Yield) and EYG, Earnings Yield Growth.

    If there are two companies with the same P/E, the one with a better PEG ratio is better. For similar logic, if two companies have the same E/P, the company with higher Earnings Growth (EPS Q/Q) would be better.
- **P/B**. Book value (= Total Assets – Total Liabilities) may not include intangible assets such as patents. Do not trust it 100%, so is ROE and other metrics which are based on the book value. Negative equity is possible when Total Liabilities is more than Total Assets. This popular metric is outdated for most matured companies as it is now made up of more intangible assets including patents, management, the quality of their employees, brand names, market share, partners, free cash flow and customer base to name a few.
- **P/S**. If two companies are unprofitable, this ratio could be more useful. A retail company such as Walmart is very different from a research company in P/S. This metric is only meaningful for stocks within the same sector or related sectors.
- **P/FCF**. I prefer it to be greater than 0 and less than 50 for value investors. Most metrics can be manipulated easily, but not this one. This is a major metric to avoid bankrupting companies.
- **Sales Q/Q** reduces the seasonal deviation. To illustrate, retail sales for the Christmas season should be compared to the same season in the prior year.
- **EPS Q/Q**. Same as above. I prefer the growth of EPS over Sales. Both of these Q/Q ratios are growth metrics. When a company terminates its unprofitable product(s), its Sales Q/Q could be down but its EPS Q/Q could be up. In 2000, many internet companies had great Sales Q/Qs but negative EPS Q/Qs.

Q/Q comparison (quarter to quarter) takes out the seasonal variations as Sales Q/Q. I prefer both Sales Q/Q and EPS Q/Q increase. When EPS Q/Q increases far higher than Sales Q/Q, it could mean the EPS Q/Q could be temporary such as the oil company when the oil price rockets.

When the company buys its own shares, EPS could be misleading as E is fixed and the number of shares is reduced. In most cases, the fundamentals of the company have not changed.

In 2021, many companies such as many energy stocks have incredible EPS Q-Q and most of their Forward P/E are better than the P/E. They could be momentum play unless they are sustainable.

- Positive **Insider** Transactions are favorable. Sometimes, they are misleading. Need to scroll to the end of the screen and check out more info there. If the transactions are outdated such as 3 months or so ago, and or they are purchases in a similar amount than the sales a while ago, they are not important. Insiders know the company better than us.

  So is **Institutional Transactions** as institutional investors move the market. Most institutional investors do not trade small stocks, and hence this metric is not important for small cap stocks.
- Insider Own, Shares Outstanding and Shares **Float** determine the number of shares that are available for trading. The stock with a small Float and a high Insider Own limits trading and the stock, and hence it should be avoided in most cases. Also, compare your trade positions for this kind of stock to their Avg. Volumes.
- **Profit Margin**. I prefer it over Gross Margin and Oper. Margin which does not include interest expenses and taxes. When you sell software, the Gross Margin is high as it does not include development, support and marketing, etc. A retail store has low Gross Margin. It all depends on the industry, and hence it is better to compare companies in the same industry.
- **Short Float**. I prefer it to be less than 10%. If it is greater than 10%, the shorters could find something wrong with the company. If it is over 25%, I would check the fundamentals and any important events such as a major lawsuit. If they are good, I would buy it expecting a short squeeze potential. It is risky but it has been proven profitable in some of my trades.
- Technical metrics: SMA-20, SMA-50 and SMA-200. Finviz expresses them in convenient percentages. If they are all positive, it means the

trend is up. SMA-20 and SMA-50 are a short-term trend indicator and SMA-200 is a long-term trend indicator. If you are a short-term swing investor, stick with the short-term trend and vice versa. The first two are also used as momentum grades. Many long-term investors do not buy stocks when the SMA-200% is negative. Some buy stocks when both SMA-20 and SMA-50 are positive and SMA-20 crosses SMA-50,. Some sell the owned stocks when both SMA-20 and SMA-50 are negative and SMA-20 crosses SMA-50. Some use SMA-50 and SMA-200 instead. They are called the Golden Cross and the Death Cross.

- **RSI(14)**. If it is greater than 65%, it is overbought to me. If it is under 30%, it is under-bought for me to me. Some use 5% up or down than my percentages. Use it as a reference. Most stocks making new heights are always overbought, and many of these stocks keep on rising. I recommend using trailing stops to protect your profits on rising stocks.
- **Beta**. A volatile stock fluctuates a lot. Higher beta stocks are good for short-term traders. A beta of 1 means the stock would fluctuate with the market, and it is more volatile if it is higher than 1. For volatile stocks (higher than 1), the stops should be higher. For example, if your stops are normally 10%, you may want to use 15% or even higher for volatile stocks.
- **Perf**. If the stock lost more than 50%, there is a good chance it could be a candidate for bottom fishing, or it could be heading to bankruptcy. Need more research if you want to buy these risky stocks.
- Management performance is measured by **ROE**. It is also judged by **Analysts' Rec.** and Institutional Ownership (except for small companies). The confidence of their own ability, the company and its sector are measured by Insider Ownership and Insider Purchases.

ROE = Net Income / Average Shareholder's Equity

According to Investopedia, a normal ROE for utilities should be 10% while high tech companies should be 15%. Compare this ratio and many other ratios with its peers that are available from many sites including Fidelity.

- Avoid all companies that are going to bankrupt at all costs. Debt/Equity, P/FCF, Cash/Sh., P/B, Profit Margin, Forward P/E, Short Float, RSI(14), SMA20% and SMA50 would give us some hints. Need to summarize all the info and study many other factors such as obsoleting products (including drugs going to be generic). Study articles which are available from Finviz and many other sites.

- Unless you have concrete information, do not buy stocks a week or so before the Earnings Date (available in Finviz). It is seldom to make great profits when the announcement is better than the expected as the stock price is usually priced in, and the reverse could hurt the stock price a lot.

More useful information:
- The price chart. It has a lot of features such as the resistance line. Some charts include technical indicators such as double top (a bearish warning) and double bottom (a bullish sign).
- Description under the symbol. It briefly describes what the company (sector and industry) does and its country of registration. You want to buy a stock within a sector that is trending up. For example, according to Finviz Apple is in the Consumer Goods sector and the Electronic Equipment industry.

    If you do not want to buy foreign stocks, skip it if it is not listed in the US exchange or headquartered in a foreign country. Buying a foreign stock could be profitable, but risky due to the currency fluctuation, lack of regulations, and politics (such as Russia in 2022 and China in 2021). Some foreign stocks ask you to pay additional taxes when you sell them. Some foreign companies listed in the U.S. exchanges take out a good portion of the dividends.
- Articles on the company for qualitative analysis.
- Insider trading. Pay more attention to the insider purchases at market prices. Use common sense.
- The last line lets you open Yahoo!Finance and other sites.

Other important sites
Yahoo!Finance.
From Statistics, you can find Enterprise Value / EBITDA. I call it True Yield when I flip them to EBITDA / Enterprise Value. In case it is not available, I use Earnings Yield. In my spreadsheet without considering the cell designations,
=IF (Earnings Yield = "", True Yield, Earnings Yield)

Fidelity
Compare the P/E of the average PE of the last 5 years by using spreadsheets.

Cheaper By Historically =IF(PE="","",(Avg. of 5-year PE -PE)/Avg. of 5-year PE)

Compare the P/E of companies in the same sector. In my spreadsheet for demonstration,
Cheaper By To the peers =IF(PE="","",(Industry PE - PE)/Industry PE)

Your broker's website

Your broker website should have plenty of tools to analyze stocks. As of Dec., 2018, Fidelity lets you use their extensive research free by opening an account with no position restriction. I describe some of their metrics that should be beneficial to your research.

- Equity Summary Score. Potentially good buy when it is 7 (8 for conservative investors) or higher. With some exceptions, you should avoid buy or short stocks if the score is 3 or below. The stocks ranking from 4 to 6 could be turnaround candidates if they are supported by good Q/Q Earnings and/or good news. The above are my suggestions.

- The 5-year averages are good yardsticks. For example, in Dec., 2018, C's P/E is about 9 and the average for the last 5 years is 14. Hence it is a value buy.

Fidelity stock research

You have to be their customer to access all their research. If you are not one already, open an account with the minimal requirements (none as of this writing) and optionally buy a no-commission ETF from them. Their research is extensive and it could be the biggest bargain. Their StarMine (Analyst Opinions) has been proven to be a good predictor to me. Your broker other than Fidelity may provide similar tools.

The following describes some of the features.

- Analyst Opinion (now Equity Summary Score). It is one of the major metrics I use in my proprietary scoring systems. They do not track a lot of small stocks. From my limited database in 7/2015 and for short durations, the results are:

Short Term: (7% return for the average)

Metric	Parm. 1	No. of Stocks	%	Parm. 2	No.	%	Predicta-bility
Fidelity Analyst	Buy	150	10%	Sell	279	3%	Good

Long Term: (8% return for the average)

Metric	Parm. 1	No. of Stocks	%	Parm. 2	No.	%	Predicta-bility
Fidelity Analyst	Buy	90	17%	Sell	208	4%	Good

- ETP (ETF to me) evaluation.
- Key Statistics. Select the industry leader by comparing the metrics to its peers. They also compare their own metrics to the average of several years. The 5-year average of P/E is useful.
- Charts for technical analysis.

Research Reports and Financial Statements give us more information about the company.

Blue Chip Growth website is no longer free. It is easy to use Fidelity to replace their grades.

Other sources

If you have other sources (most require a subscription or being a customer), skip the stocks that have one of the failing grades. The exceptions are a new positive development and increased insider purchases.

Vendor	Grade	Fail
Fidelity	Equity Summary Score	< 7
IBD	Composite grade	< 50
Value Line	Proj. 3-5 yr. return. Also, its composite rating	< 3%
Zacks	Rank	5
VectorVest	VST	< 0.7

You may be able to find Value Line and IBD in your local library. Try out the free stock reports from your broker first. Finviz and Seeking Alpha should have articles (now fewer free articles from Seeking Alpha) on stocks and earnings conferences, which could have important information after separating from the "welcome" and garbage talks.

Yahoo!Finance has good info. "EV/EBITDA" is better than "P/E" as it considers debts and cash. Most use Earnings from the last 12 months, which has poorer predictability than Forward Earnings to me.

When negative values such as Equity in Finviz.com, we need to adjust many related metrics or do not use them at all.

MarketWatch.com has many articles on the market in general and personal investing.

If the stock is close to the Earnings Date (found in Finviz.com), you should avoid trading the stock; as earnings could have a big swing for the stock price. Consult Zacks' ranking which is currently free for individual stocks.

Gurus

It is nice to know how gurus would rate the interested stocks. GuruFocus is a good source but requires subscription. NASDAQ is a simplified version. Bring up Nasdaq.com from your browser. Select "Investing" and then "Guru Screeners". On the third selection, enter the stock symbol such as THO. Click "Go". You will find how 10 or so gurus would evaluate this stock in theory. Click "Detailed Analysis" for each guru.

Quick and dirty

Many times we need to evaluate a stock fast such as taking action due to some development. Or, when you have over 30 stocks from your screen, you may want to reduce the number by using the following two methods.

Refer to my other article "Simplest way to evaluate stocks". The following should take a few minutes. Bring up Finviz.com and enter the stock symbol.

Using SWKS on 6/10/16 to illustrate, Forward P/E is about 11 (fine between 3 and 25), Debt/Eq. is 0 (fine less than .5), ROE is 30% (fine greater than 5%) and P/PCF is 31 (fine if not negative).

Also, check out Market Cap, Avg. Volume, Dividend, Short Float (fine between 0% and 10%), Country and Industry. Judging from the above, it is a buy.

If you have more time, check out the following: Recom. (Ok if less than 2.5), P/B (fine between .5 and 4), Sales Q/Q (fine if not negative), EPS Q/Q (fine if not negative), Cash/Sh (compare it to Debt/Sh) and Profit Margin (fine >5%). Check some articles described for this stock.

5-minute stock evaluation
It takes even less time than the above "Quick and Dirty". However, I recommend you should spend more time researching stocks.

- From Finviz.com, enter the stock or ETF symbol. Look at the number of reds in metrics. If there are more than greens, most likely it is not a good stock.
- It should be fine if Fidelity's Equity Summary Score is greater than 8.

If you have more time, I recommend you to check the following:

- Check out Forward P/E (E>0 and P/E < 20), Debut / Equity (< 50%) and P/FCF (not in red color).

  If time is allowed, replace Forward P/E with True P/E (same as "EV/EBITDA"), which is available from Yahoo!Finance and other sources.
- SMA20 (or SMA50 for longer holding period). If SMA20 is > 10%, it is trending up.
- It is fine if the Insider Transaction is positive.
- Be cautious on foreign stocks and low-volume stocks.
- If most of the above are positive, it is likely a buy. As in life, nothing is 100% certain.

Links
PEG: http://en.wikipedia.org/wiki/PEG_ratio
Short %: http://www.investopedia.com/university/shortselling/shortselling1.asp#axzz2LNDvpemo
Openinsider: http://www.openinsider.com/
Finviz: http://Finviz.com/
terms: http://www.Finviz.com/help/screener.ashx
Insider Cow: http://www.insidercow.com/
Current Ratio: http://en.wikipedia.org/wiki/Current_ratio
Cash Flow: https://www.youtube.com/watch?v=1v8hRZ36--c
Balance sheet: https://www.youtube.com/watch?v=DZjU0CHKyV4
How to find quality stocks.

http://seekingalpha.com/article/2381395-how-to-identify-quality-stocks-and-is-there-really-alpha-to-be-had

3   Intangibles

I give a score for each stock I evaluate. Occasionally some stocks with poor scores have great returns and vice versa. In general, the scoring system works. It has been proven statistically and repeatedly from my limited data. I stick with high-score stocks with some exceptions.

Once in a while I change my scoring system to adapt to the current market conditions. To illustrate, the market bottom phase and early recovery phase of the market cycle favor value more than momentum/growth. Here are some of my recent experiences and strategies:

- I double or even triple my stake on stocks with high scores. In the longer term, they are consistently better winners than the average with some minor exceptions. Besides the score, look at the intangibles described in this article.

- Watch out for the stocks with outrageous metrics such as P/E of 4 or less. It could be a big lawsuit pending, an expiration of some important drugs, etc. Also, be careful with scores in the top 5%. From my statistics they do worse than the average. Their problems may not show up in the current financial statements.

- The technology of a tech company cannot be ignored even though the company's P/E is high, that I set a limit of 25 instead of 20 for other stocks. The value of the company's technology and patents will not be shown in the fundamental metrics except from the insiders' purchases at market prices.

    For example, IDCC rose about 40% in 2 days. There was a rumor that Google was buying the company and/or Apple was bidding on it too for its mobile technology. Charts usually would flag this kind of event. For non-charters, use the SMA-20% from Finviz.com. They could be a little late as the charts depend on rising prices.

- There are more acquisitions during a market bottom (same as early recovery). The companies with good technologies are bargains and the larger companies especially those in the same sector understand their values better than most of us. These potentially profitable companies will not be shown by their scores explicitly. When corporations have a lot of cash or the credit is cheap, they are looking for smaller companies to acquire or invest in. The candidates are usually small, beaten up, low-priced and having valuable intangible assets such as technologies, customer base and/or market share of the industry segment. 2009-2012 was just the perfect environment and the before that was 2003. I had at least one stock in each of these periods and they appreciated a lot.

- The opposite is Netflix, Chipotle in 1/2012 and Amazon in 1/2013. They are overpriced by any measure. However, the mentioned companies are investing in the future. The shorters (not for beginners) are having a tough time making money on them. When their P/Es are higher than 40, watch out. Some could be OK in the mentioned companies, but usually they are not. Do not follow the herd and your due diligence will verify whether they will still go up.

  Use reward/risk ratio. It is based on experiences. To illustrate, if the company has the equal chance to go up 50% and go down 25%, then it is a buy and the reverse is a sell.

- The retail investor just cannot possibly know about some events until they actually happen. For example, ATSC dropped 15% due to losing its second primary customer. Fundamentals cannot predict this kind of event. Charts can signal this event, but usually they are too late unless you watch the chart all day long.

- After a quick run up, TZOO plunged due to missing some negligible earning expectations. It seems the original climbing prices already had the perfect earnings growth built-in.

  I do not understand why a company loses 10% of its market cap when it missed by 1% of the expected earnings. It could be driven up and down by the institutional investors. Evaluate the stock before you act. Acting opposite to the institutional investors could be very profitable for the right stocks. Avoid trading before the earnings announcement dates (about 4 times a year for most stocks).

- The following are not easily found in financial statements: industry outlook, patents, good will, market share, competition, product margins, management quality, lawsuits pending, potential acquisition, pension obligations, advertising icons, etc. That is why we need to read articles on the stocks in our buy list or our purchased stocks.

- The financial data could be fraudulent or manipulated. I do not trust small companies in emerging markets. I have been burned too many times. Check the company names such as foreign names, ADR and their headquarter addresses (from the company profile in most investing sites).

  Earnings can be manipulated with many accounting tricks. A jump in earnings from last year may not be as rosy as it looks. Check the footnotes in the accounting statements. I usually skip financial statements unless I have big purchases in mind as my time in investing is limited.

- Cash flow cannot be easily manipulated. It is good information whether the company will survive or not, but to me it does not prove to be a consistent predictor in my tests, but an important red flag for companies on their way to bankruptcy. Examples abound.

- Repeated one-time, non-recurring and extraordinary charges are red flags.

- Stay away from the companies where the CEOs are over-compensated. As of 7- 2013, Activision's CEO raised his salary by more than 600%, while the stock lost its value in double digits.

- Value stocks. Need to know why they become value stocks (i.e., fewer investors want to own them) even if they are fundamentally sound. For example, there are two primary reasons for the downfall of a supplier to Apple: 1. Apple is declining in sales and 2. Apple is switching suppliers to replace their product. Technology companies are continually building better mouse traps. They could turn around in a year or so with better products.

Conclusion

Buying a stock is an educated guess that its stock price will rise. Fundamentals do not always work, but they work most of the time:

1. When we buy a value stock, we're swimming against the tide. Hence, we need to wait longer (usually more than 6 months) for the market to realize its value. The exception is the Early Recovery phase (see the

Market Cycle chapter) and it has faster and larger returns than most other stocks from most other stages of the market cycle.

2. Some metrics are misleading. Book value could be misleading for an established company such as IBM. The image of the cowboy in a tobacco company could be a very important asset that is not included in its financial statement.

3. The market is not always rational.

Afterthoughts

- Brand names of big companies are one of the most important intangibles. Here is a strategy to buy big companies in a down market. It has been proven that it works. However, do not just buy these companies without analysis.
http://seekingalpha.com/article/1324041-buying-brand-names-in-a-bear-market-can-make-you-rich

- The reputation of a company takes a long time to build but a bad incident to destroy in the case of GM such as the delay in recalling the killer switches.

#Filler: Carrie Fisher, another sad American story

Unless drug addiction is part of the culture now as evidenced from the legalization of certain drugs, we're in a permissive society! Brits pushed opium as a nation when they had nothing better to trade. Opium killed millions of Chinese and bankrupted China. When we do not learn from history, we will repeat history. It is another sad story of fame and money and then losing it all. I bet she would be happier in a normal life instead of being born in a privileged class. Same can be said for many celebrities such as Presley, Houston and her daughter. RIP.

4   Qualitative analysis

This is the last analysis to evaluate a stock fundamentally. Then the next is technical analysis which is used to find an entry point (also the exit point) for the stock. The market is not always rational. It also depends on the available of money such as easy credit to pump up the market.

Where quantitative analysis fails and why

I find that some stocks with high scores fail and some stocks with low scores succeed as indicated by my performance monitor. The scoring system still works statistically for the majority of my stocks.

- Reasons why stocks with low scores perform:

    o Oversold. The institutional investors (fund managers and pension managers) dump them first, and then followed by the retail investors. These big boys will buy these stocks back when they reach a certain price range. RSI(14), a technical indicator described in the Technical Analysis article and is available from many sites including Finviz, is useful to detect these oversold stocks.

    o The falling price (P) improves all fundamental metrics that have the stock price such as P/E and P/Sales. However, the trend of the price is down. Improving Forward P/E is usually a good hint.

    o The company has turned around after fixing its problems and/or the market has changed for the better. A new management team could improve profitability such as recalling Steve Jobs for Apple.

    o The current problems have been resolved but not known to the public that could be evidenced by the increase in Insiders' Purchases (from Finviz to start). It includes resolving a lawsuit, a new product, a new drug, or a new big order, etc.

    o Heavy purchases by insiders. The company's outlook is not shown in its financial statements. Sometimes the insiders hide them so they can buy more of their companies' stocks for themselves.

- Reasons why stocks with high scores plunge in addition to the described in the previous discussion:

- The company's fundamentals and its prices have reached or closed to the maximum heights. They have no way to go but down. It is particularly true when the stock's timing rating is at or close to the highest point. TTWO that I gifted to my grandchildren had been 5-baggers in the last few years before it plunged in 2018.

- It has reached its potential value (or a target price) and it is time for many investors to take profits.

- Sector (or finding another stock or sector with better appreciation potential)) rotation, particularly by institutional investors who drive the market.

    - The outlook of the company, its sector and/or the market is deteriorating. Most companies with P/E less than 5 have problems, and you need to find out the reasons why the stocks are so cheap. Via Finviz, check out debt / share (more than 0.5), negative Q-Q Sales, negative Q-Q Profits, and/or outdated products like typewriters.

- The stock price may be manipulated. There are many reasons to pump and dump the stock. Shorting is not recommended for most investors. However, some experienced shorters make money consistently when they find valid reasons to short stocks.

- It could be due to a new serious lawsuit, a new competing product or drug, canceling a major order, etc.

- Downgrade by analysts. They could spot some bad events such as product defects, violations of regulations or accounting errors / frauds. The downgrades are more important than the upgrades that could have conflict of interest.
- The financial statement had been manipulated. The SEC may ask for an investigation.
- Does not meet the consensus in earnings announcements, which have been over-acted by many investors.

Qualitative Analysis

We need to do further analysis after the quantitative analysis and the intangible analysis. Check out the company's prospects. Check out the date of the article and any potential hidden agenda items from the author. Older articles may not have much value.

Be careful on 'pump-and-dump' manipulation written by authors with a hidden agenda. It has happened especially on small companies before even SeekingAlpha.com has its share. Here was an article that tells you to sell NHTC. There was another article to tell you to buy ARTX. They fit into this category.

The sources are:

1. Seeking Alpha.
   Type the symbol of the company to read as many articles on the company as you have time for. Today this site and many other similar sites require you to be a paid member. If you cannot find too many good articles, check out the articles from Finviz.com.

   Recently, I read an article on AMD and it said it may have good profits in the next two years with the game consoles. The outlook of a company is not shown by any fundamental metric which are far from favorable.

   Following a well-known writer, I bought IBM without doing my due diligence (my fault). It went down more than 15% quickly. You can learn from my mistakes.
2. Research reports from your broker. If you do not find many, open an account with one that provides such reports. Some subscription services such as Value Line provide such reports.
3. Yahoo!Finance board. Most comments are garbage. However, once in a while you find some great insights. Usually, you cannot find any info from other sources on tiny companies.
4. The most recent company's financial statements. They are usually available from the company's website.
5. 10-Ks from Edgar database (www.sec.gov/edgar). Check out new products and its potential competition, key customers, order backlog, research and development and pending lawsuits.
6. Check out the outlook of the sector the company is in and the company itself.
7. Check out its competitors.

8. Some companies are run by stupid people. I received information via my email saying that my mutual fund account could be treated as an abandoned property. I have been cashing dividend checks every year and why it would be considered as an abandoned property. I called them right away to close my account.

    The tall and handsome guy presented articulately how he would turn around JC Penny on TV. I could tell you right away that all his tricks had been tried by other companies such as Sears, and most did not work. The intelligent investor does not care about how handsome, how articulate, how rich his family is and how many advanced degrees from prestigious colleges he possesses. If he does not make sense, do not buy his preaching and his company's stock. [Update. As of 5/2020, J.C. Penny filed for bankruptcy protection. If you had this stock and my book, you would have saved a lot of money minus $10 for my book!]

9. Check out its business model. Some business models do not make business sense and some do. Here are some samples.
- Giving razors makes sense, as the customers have to buy the blades eventually and keep on buying blades for life.
- Supermarket M lowers prices on common merchandise such as Coke and it works. They make money by providing inferior (but profitable to them) products that you cannot compare prices easily such as meat and seafood.

    Eventually there will be a supermarket in my area to satisfy me both in price and quality or at least make a good tradeoff.
- Last week it had been brutally hot. I went to a Barnes & Noble's bookstore to enjoy reading the updated books and enjoyed the air conditioning. When there are more free loaders like me than customers, this business model does not work.
- Market dumping works to capture the market. Microsoft used to do it with their new Office and Mail products that could not compete with the established products at the time. Google is following the same model to dump its equivalent products to compete with Office. Now, Microsoft is taking a dose of the same medicine. As of 2015, Google is not winning.

5   Sectors to be cautious with

There are many reasons to be very cautious when investing in the following sectors. However, Technical Analysis (a.k.a. charting) would give you more hints than the fundamentals for stocks for these sectors. If the big guys are dumping, most likely Technical Analysis (or the simplest SMA-20) would tell you that.

Loan companies/banks

The financial statements do not show the quality of their loan portfolios. Following this advice, you may be able to skip the banks that melted down in 2007. The peak of Citigroup is $550 and several banks went bankrupt.

Drug (generic is ok)

Understanding the complexities of the drug pipelines, its potential profits for new drugs and the expiration of the current drugs may not worth the effort for most retail investors. In addition, a serious lawsuit and / or a serious problem with a drug could wipe out a good percentage of the stock price. When a drug shows unpromising sign(s) in any trial phase, the stock could plunge and vice versa.

Miners

It is extremely difficult to estimate how much ore (sometimes a miner owns several different types of ores and/or of different grades in the same or different mines) that a company has. It is further complicated by the complexities to extract and transport them. When the total of these costs is greater than its production price, the company will not be profitable. Understanding the market for ore futures is another discipline.

Many mining companies are in foreign countries such as Canada, Australia and countries in South America. Their financial statements of Canada and Australia are more trustworthy than most other emerging countries.

One potential problem of mining companies from many emerging countries is nationalization.

Mining rare earth ore is extremely risky when the profit depends on how China, a major producer of these ores, will price these ores. After China announced the export restrictions on rare earth elements, several non-Chinese companies announced to reopen their mines for rare earths, but few have made any profits as of 2013. Developed countries have stricter environmental regulations.

Coal and eventually oil suffer from the rising use of cleaner energy such as solar and wind.

Insurance companies

Insurance companies profit by:

1. The difference between the total premiums received and the total claims minus expenses in running the company.
2. How well they invest the premiums; you pay your premiums earlier than you may collect from any claims.

They can protect the profits in #1 by restricting claims by natural disasters such as earthquakes and by re-insuring. However, a bad disaster could wipe out a lot of their profits.

Even if the insurance company shows you its investment portfolio, most of us, the retail investors, do not have the time and expertise to analyze it.

Emerging countries (not a sector)
Their financial statements especially from small companies cannot be trusted, and many countries use different accounting standards. Emerging countries are where the economic growth is. I trade FXI, an ETF, rather than individual Chinese companies. I have lost a lot in small Chinese companies due to frauds and politics. To check out whether the stock is an ADR, try ADR.COM (https://www.adr.com/).

Stocks with low volumes (not a sector)
Most likely you pay a high spread to trade these stocks. They can be manipulated easier. I had a hard time trying to sell a stock owned by a few owners.

For simplicity, I trade stocks with the average daily trade volume over 6,000 shares (double it if the price is $2 or less). A better way could be by calculating the percent of your trade quantity / average daily trade volume;

it would reduce the effect of penny stocks that have larger volumes due to the low prices.

Good business and bad business

Banking is a good business in a growing economy. My deposit in them makes virtually zero interest, and they loan the same money making 3%. If they are more cautious in loaning, they should make good profits.

Restaurant is an easy business to run, but it is very hard to make good money. With the rising of minimal wages, it will get even tougher. That could be the reason for so many coupons today. The high-end restaurants are doing better due to the rising stock market. The pandemic of 2020 would wipe out a lot of small restaurants.

Retailing is a tough business. Look at the top 10 retailers 15 years ago, I can only find two including Macy's that are still surviving. Most are either went bankrupt or being acquired. Even Macy's was not in good financial shape. Amazon is the killer.

Airlines are a tough business. You can tell by the average increase in fares in the last 10 years. It cannot even beat inflation. They have to charge you for everything. The next frontier charge is the rest room (especially for long-distance flights). Now I understand why they call themselves "Frontier Air". As of 2014, it is quite profitable due to mergers and lower fuel cost. The pandemic of 2020 may be the toughest time for airlines. As of 5/2020, Boeing has many serious troubles and they can only survive with a bailout from the government.

There are several software companies that produce software such as the virus detecting programs and tax preparation software. The customers faithfully buy new versions every year. That's great business.

6 A scoring system

My scoring system in my book Scoring Stocks described in more detail helps me to select whether you should buy a stock or not. In that system, when a stock scores higher than 2, it is a buy. As a group, the highly-scored stocks usually perform better than the lowly-scored stocks over many years. I describe the basic concept here and see some real examples later.

An Example

For illustration, we use three metrics: expected P/E, ROI and the percentile of the ROI to its industry (from 0% to 100%).

First we convert P/E into E/P. Assuming E/P should have a higher weight than ROI, multiply it by 5. The average Percentile is 50%, so minus it by .5.

Score = E/P * 5 + ROI + (Percentile -.5)

For example, a stock has a P/E of 10 (E/P = 1/10= .1) and ROI is expressed as 25% and it is 60% percentile (better than 40 of its peers).

Score = .1 * 5 + .25 + (.6 - .5) = .5 + .25 + .1 = .85

Where ROI is expressed as a number instead of a percentage, divide it by 100.

Some parameters are expressed in grade such as A, B, C and D. For simplicity, if it is A, then the value is 5 otherwise it is zero.

Score = if (Grade = "A", 5, 0) + ...

Test your system on paper with at least 3 months of data. Check whether your scoring system works. It works when the higher the score corresponds to the better the return. Adjust the weight on each metric and see whether the scoring system improves its predictability.

Again, it is simplified for educational and illustration purpose. Try more different metrics and check whether the metrics still work in the current market.

Monitor your scoring system

I am sure that many have tried to use most of the metrics and they still cannot find the Holy Grail. I believe the predictability power of each metric is influenced by the current market conditions. For example, the fundamental metrics (P/E...) predict better than the growth metrics (PEG...) during the market bottom. You should test the performance of each metric every 6 months as mentioned.

You may have two scores: one for short term and one for long term. The stocks you want to keep in the short term may not be the same kind of stocks you want to keep in the longer term. Short term is 3 months and long term is 12 months for me. My definitions could be different from yours.

However, 12 months is too long a period and during this period the market may change, so you may want to change it from 12 to 6. To illustrate, energy stocks were great in 2007, but they plunged in 2008. If your scoring system for long-term holding was constructed based on 12 months' data in 2007, the system would be misleading in 2008 at least for energy stocks in this example.

I find the short-term scores have better prediction power than the long-term scores. However, I keep some stocks longer term to qualify for the better tax treatments in taxable accounts. One solution is to evaluate the purchased stocks every 6 months to decide whether to sell it or keep it for another 6 months.

Besides monitor the metrics in your scoring system, monitor the scores. I recommend have two scoring systems: one for short term and one for long term. Value metrics are more important for long term while growth metrics are more important for the short term.

The market is not always rational

Sometimes the scoring system fails: When the poorly-scored stocks perform better than the highly-scored stocks. The market is not always rational. Most scoring systems depend on fundamental metrics. When the market switches its favor from value to growth, adjust the score system accordingly. I find more than one time that the stocks scored in the top 5% do not perform, so be careful or skip the top 5% (sometimes 10%). My guess is they may have something not found in the metrics such as a pending lawsuit or an expiring drug – some call it value trap.

Some metrics always work such as Insider's Purchase. The insiders know the company typically better than others. When they buy their own company's stock at the market prices, they must know it has good appreciation potential. They have many reasons to sell its company's stock. However, when they sell a large percent of their holdings, be worry.

When the stock loses more than 30% in a month and you cannot find valid reasons, it may be a good indicator for potential appreciation ahead. Some suggestions are:

- Do not modify your scoring system during market plunges.
- The best strategy is to use the screens (same as searches) that work for the last 90 days.
- Find out why your fundamental metrics that used to work do not work now. You may want to add more weight on growth metrics and vice versa on value metrics.

Afterthoughts

This is what I found in monitoring the performances of the metrics as of 3/2013. It is based on a limited database of about 300 stocks with holding periods varying from 1 to 15 months. It has an average of 8% (16% for shorter term). The following is for educational purpose only.

1. The foreign stocks are not doing well: South America (average return is -21% for 7 stocks), Israel (-18% for 2), China (-10% for 7). Europe (0% for 17) and Canada (5% for 16, and most in natural resources). If I ignore the foreign companies, the return of the portfolio would be increased substantially.

2. The following metrics work fine in the long term only: expected earning yield (E/P) and Fidelity's Analysts' Opinion.

3. P/B. The stocks with P/B less than 1 perform better than the stocks with P/B greater than 2 (10% vs. 4%).

4. There are no conclusive conclusions on Cash / Market Cap, PEG and Return of Equity (a surprise to me) in this monitor.

5. The stocks cheaper by 50% to its average 5-year P/E performs better than those stocks cheaper by less than 2%.

6. The ratio of Short / Market Cap between 25% and 30% has best performance than other percentages. It is a contradictory ratio and it could be short squeezes (a condition that the stock is running out of shared to sell short).

7. There are many composite scores from different vendors that I subscribe and they are not disclosed here. Hence in practice, my scoring system is not the same as described here.

8. Based on the above, I will modify my score system. Will still have two scores, one for short term and one for long term.

Short-term scoring system

The score system should work better in the shorter term. I used the above database but deleted stocks that have been over 8 months old. It is still a small database of about 190 stocks. The metrics are from different sources, so it is not possible to use a historical database from one vendor for my testing. For example, my vendor's historical database does not include IBD's composite grade.

The result is different from the above as the time frame is reduced. Here is the summary.

1. The predictability of screens (same as searches) performs about the same as the last monitor. A few screens are better than others. Will not use the under-performed screens for real money.

2. The value composite scores from several vendors are not a good indicator this time.

3. Expected earning yield (E/P) should be a good indicator.

4. Cash Flow is a good indicator (different from the last monitor).

5. Fidelity's Analysts' Opinion is a good indicator. If you do not have access to it, it is available in similar forms from many other sources such as Finviz. Fidelity selects higher weight on opinions from analysts that have better prediction on this stock before. It eliminates some of the conflict of interest between the analyst and its investing banks s/he works for.

6. The Short Percentage between 25 and 30 is a good contrary indicator (could be a good chance for short squeeze).

   Its value of less than 10 % is a good indicator. The rest of the range is not conclusive.

7. Cash / Market Cap, Insider Purchase, P/B, ROE and Dividend stocks (>3%) are not conclusive in this monitor.

8. P/S with values less than 0.8 is a good indicator.

9. For some reason I do not know why and how to explain, the top 10% of the top-scored stocks do not perform better than the other stocks that pass. It happens in both my two scoring systems. Be suspicious on them and it has happened for more than one time. The stocks scored in the bottom 10% are consistently poor performers and that's good.

There are many other parameters that may be interested to you. Include them in the performance monitor.

7   Examples of overpriced stocks

In 2011, there were discussions on the high valuation of Netflix in several articles in Seeking Alpha, an investment website. LinkedIn and Facebook shares were believed to be overvalued even before their IPOs.

Here are some of my thoughts on Netflix and the same concept can be applied to other stocks.

- Reward / Risk ratio.
  If the stock has the same probability to move up by 30% and move down by 50%, it is overvalued by 20% (50% - 30%). As of 2011, Netflix shares may rise, but it is too risky for me.
- Compare the P/E to its five-year average.
  The current P/E is 60 and the average for the last 5 years is 30. From this metric it is overvalued by 100%.

  The 'E' in P/E can be either expected (same as forward) earnings or based on the last 12 months (same as trailing or historical). It has been proven that the 'expected' is a better indicator than the 'historical'. AAII demonstrated this by comparing the performances of the expected PEG screen and the historical PEG screens over a long period of time.
- Fools who invested in the high P/E stocks and did not do their due diligence in 2000 had parted with their money fast. I could not convince my friends to take money off their internet stocks. It is similar to asking the lottery winners not to buy lottery tickets.
- Buying an expensive stock is like over paying for a hot dog cart in NYC for $100,000. The buyer will sell many hot dogs, but the rate of return of the investment will be minimal, and it will never recover the initial investment. "Buy high and sell higher" is a momentum play. It works if it is played with stops, but I prefer to "Buy low and sell high".
- Following a decent and proven investing strategy consistently should lead to success through persistence and adjustments. In the long term, a bad strategy always loses money.
- When the market favors growth / momentum (vs. value), it is OK to buy stocks with prices higher than the intrinsic values by a small percentage. The tide is on your side. However, be attentive to any indication that the market is changing direction.
- NFLX has an average annual return rate of 177% vs. SPY's 14% from 1/3/2011 to 1/3/2020 without considering dividends. Hence, a trailing stop would do the job for the rocket stock.

8 Avoid bankrupting companies

Avoid the bankrupting companies at all costs. Here are some hints that a company is going bankrupt:

- I had several companies that had lost most of their stock values. It turns out that most were Chinese companies. I did have some losers from Mexico, Israel and Ireland. I believe most were set up to cheat investors. Most if not all had 'rosy' financial statements. Avoid them, especially small companies in emerging countries.
- Many U.S. companies failed due to fraud, poor management, and/or the management betting wrongly. When the CEO is using the company as his own AMT, or having an extravagant lifestyle, watch out. If they promise you a return doubling the current rate of return of the market, listen to your wise mother: there is no free lunch. Despite so many real examples, still fools are born every day, because greed is a human nature.
- Do not follow the 'commentators' on TV. They have their own hidden agenda which usually is not in your interest.
- Many companies fail due to their lack of ability to pay back their loans. Except for specific industries and situations, avoid companies with high debt (Debt/Equity over 50%). Financial institutions and companies that have high debt in order to finance their products for their customers such as utilities are the exceptions.
- I have a screen named Big Losers beating the market by more than 600% in Early Recovery (a phase defined by me). However, some bankrupt companies are not included in the database which is termed as survivor bias. Hence, the actual result is far worse than the 600%. I still use this screen but skip these companies using the following yardsticks.
    - The companies are usually safe with high Free Cash Flow / Equity and high Expected Profit / Stock Price.
    - The following are red flags: low Free Cash Flow / Equity, high Inventory and high Receivable (esp. relative to its Payable), high P/B (over 30) and high net Debt/Equity (over 1 to 3 depending on the industry).
    - P/PFC should be greater than 0 and less than 50. A healthy cash flow may not be able to service the debt if it is too huge. Hence, compare it to Debt/Equity. Compare the cash flow per year to debt obligations per year.
- New government regulations could bankrupt an industry. What would happen when the U.S. takes out the rebates and subsidies of solar

panels? When the U.S. banned solar panels from China, one of my Chinese stocks went bankrupt. Also, the government bailed out bankrupt companies such as Chrysler (that I made a good profit from) and AIG Fannie Mae in 2008.
- Serious lawsuits- Most U.S. companies are required to file this information in their financial reports.
- Obsolete products. Newspapers, retail and similar products would be replaced by the internet. The opposite is new products such as virtual reality products.
- Many companies run out of money during the development phase of the major products. Many are too optimistic in their business plans.
- If you expect the market will recover in 2 years, ensure the company's cash and net income can support their burn rate for at least two more years.
- Many investing sites (most require subscriptions) have safety scores.
- If the Beneish M-Score is greater than -2.22, the company is likely an accounting manipulator.
- Choose companies with Z-Score higher than 3; it is not applicable to financial companies. Both M-Score and Z-Score are available from GuruFocus, a paid subscription. Z-Score does not work for financial institutions.
- Z-Score metrics are: "Working Capital / Total Assets" (A), "Retained Earnings / Total Assets" (B), "Earnings Before Interest & Taxes / Total Assets" (C), "Market Cap / Total Liabilities" (D) and "Sales / Total Assets" (E).
Z-Score = 1.2 A + 1.4 B + 3.3 C + .6 D + E
- Market timing- It does not always work, but it is far better to follow a proven technique than not. It is far safer to take money out of the market when the market is too risky or is plunging. The big losers are companies that provide non-essential products in a downturn.
- Small companies could be risky but very profitable. Typically, they have a low stock price (less than $5), small market cap (less than 50 M), low sales (less than $25 M) and low institutional ownership (less than 5%).
- Avoid companies when their own bond ratings are not equal to AAA or AA (www.moodys.com).
- The fall of a sector such as oil in 2015 could drive the related companies, or even a country to the brink of bankruptcy.

Investing is risky to start with. However, investing especially in stocks has been proven to be the best vehicle to beat inflation.

9 Technical analysis (TA)

The basics

Technical analysis (a.k.a. charting) is easier to learn than expected. It represents the trend of the market (a stock or a group of stocks) graphically. If more investors are in the market, a stock or a group of stocks, its trend is up until it changes. We divide the trends into short-term, intermediate-term and long-term.

The chartists usually do not consider fundamentals as they believe they have already been priced in the stock price and some fundamentals are not available to the public. To illustrate, a new drug has been discovered, the stock price of the company jumps initially by insiders and the informed. Its fundamental metrics do not show right away but many are buying to boost up the stock price.

The volume is a confirmation. When the stock moves up or down by 10% with a low volume, the trend is not confirmed.

The trend of the stock price is not straight line in most cases. Hence a trend line is usually drawn to indicate the direction of the stock. Many believe the stocks fluctuate in certain range (i.e. channels) and the chart draws the upper value (the resistance line) and the lower value (the support line).

When the price passes the channel, it is called a breakout. Darvas, one of the oldest and successful chartists, profited from the breakouts of the resistance line and believed the stock is close to the support line of the new channel. Hence it has a long way up.

If it is so simple, there will be no poor folks

It works most of the time, but do not bet all your money on it. For chartists, 51% is great (same for playing Black Jack). Some trends reverse very fast such as the bio drug stocks in 2015. You need to hedge your bets such as placing stop orders. Most do not want to spend their lives in watching the trend from a big screen. Most novices use too many technical indicators and lose to the professionals.

Simple Moving Average
The basic technical indicator is SMA-N. It is the average of the last N trade sessions. When N is 20 (or SMA-20), we classify it as short-term. Similarly,

SMA-50 is intermediate-term and SMA-200 is long-term. I prefer 50, 100 and 250. This trend duration is important. For example, you do not want to place long-term bets using SMA-50 uptrend. There are many modifications to SMA that I do not find them better such as giving more weights to recent data. Finviz.com includes this information without charting.

Defining the trend periods is arbitrary. I use SMA-350 to detect market plunges and SMA-100 for stocks.

Trend is your best friend

Most use TA for trending for short durations. Investors can also use TA to time the entry and exit points for better potential profits. Value investors usually are patient and they do bottom fishing and they search for 'oversold' condition using RSI(14). Again high volume is a confirmation.

Many sites provide charting free of charge such as Yahoo!Finance. Finviz.com provides a lot of technical indicators without charting such as SMA% and RSI(14). It also provides screen searching for stocks that meet your technical analysis criteria.

TA patterns

There are many TA patterns such as Bollinger Bands and MACD. The patterns are based on the stock prices and many times they prove correct predictions especially on stocks with high volumes and high market caps.

10   More on technical analysis

This chapter describes some TA indicators that can help us. Click on the links for better description.

- Finviz.com.
  It has SMA20, SMA50 and SMA200 to represent the short-term, intermediate-term and the long-term indicator. SMA stands for Simple Moving Average and n for days for the duration of the average (for example, 20 days for SMA20).

  If you are a long-term investor, use SMA-200 (or SMA-350). Using SMA-20 would cause a lot of sells / reentries.

  Buy when the price is above the moving average line and sell when the price is below it. Finviz.com provides the percent of moving above the moving average to indicate how much the price deviates from the average.

  If you hold the stock for an average of 50 days, use SMA50, and so on. If you hold stocks for an average of 90 days, you have to create your own SMA using one of the many websites including Yahoo!Finance and specify 90 for the period.

  Try other similar technical indicators such as EMA, which is supposed to weigh more on the more recent data. A weather man can predict tomorrow's weather better than the weather a week away.

- RSI(14) indicates whether the stock is overbought or oversold. RSI oscillates between zero and 100. Traditionally, and according to Wilder, RSI is considered overbought with a value above 70 and oversold with a value below 30 as described in the article.

  When it is oversold, most likely the stock will fall, and vice versa.

(http://stockcharts.com/school/doku.php?id=chart_school:technical_indicators:relative_strength_index_rsi)

   Click here for another article.
(http://financial-dictionary.thefreedictionary.com/Relative+Strength+Index)

- Cup and handle is a popular indicator that the stock price would surge.
  (http://www.investopedia.com/terms/c/cupandhandle.asp)

- Double bottom indicates that the stock will move up.
  (http://stockcharts.com/school/doku.php?id=chart_school:chart_analysis:chart_patterns:double_bottom_revers)

  It shows a double bottom for Apple in 2013.

  The reverse is double top.

- Most indicators can be used on a market ETF to predict the market direction. It can use a sector ETF to predict a sector such as housing.

- Fidelity has a software system named Wealth Lab available free to qualified customers to test technical indicators with a historical database for back testing. Check the current availability.

- TA usually does not spot the bottoms/peaks predictably, but the trend. To me, it is more profitable to understand 4 technical indicators fully than more than 4. The four indicators to me are SMA (EMA), RSI(14), MACD and candlestick. You can also detect market change by using RSI and MACD.

  http://www.youtube.com/watch?v=adSGUkNX5LA

- It could be one profitable strategy to trade stocks with heavy insider's purchases. The dumping by institutional investors is obvious when the price moved down with heavy volume. However, insiders are human too and they could be wrong sometimes.

11   An example on technical analysis

I have outlined how we can spot market plunge using TA and I use it to monitor the market every three months or so (recommend to do it every month and even more often when the market is risky). Here is an example on how to use it to trade individual stocks.

I have to admit I do not use TA that much on individual stocks and clearly I am not an expert in TA. If this article stirs up your interest, read more books or attend seminars / classes on TA. However, this book describes the basic and most useful technical indicators. There are many good and free articles from Investopedia on this topic. Personally I prefer to seek fundamentally sound companies at bargain prices and wait for their full appreciation. It has been proven to me.

TA is very useful for momentum and day traders. With the rising volumes, you can detect that the stocks are traded by managers of mutual funds, hedge funds, insurance companies and pension funds, and profit by riding on their wagons.

Some stocks are good for TA. Usually they are larger companies with above-average volumes and are fundamentally sound. Avoid the stocks that are trending downwards unless you're bottom fishing. Let me pick CSCO (a cyclical stock) for illustration. I bought it several times in 2012. I sold some in 2013 and 2014 making good profits. This is quite different from what short-term traders would use the following information for.

The green line is 50-day simple moving average (SMA) for the following chart using one year data.

If it does not display clearly on a small screen, type the following on the browser on your PC.

http://ebmyth.blogspot.com/2013/05/chart-for-ta-example.html

Buy the stock when it is above its SMA and sell when it is below. Following the chart would make good money based on this simple rule. Also, practice the strategy "Sell on May 1, Buy back on Nov. 1".

Not all stocks follow this profitable pattern. Fundamentalists may try to pick the bottom in late July while chartists enter positions on its upward trend. The chartists have an advantage to stay away from stocks in their downward trend.

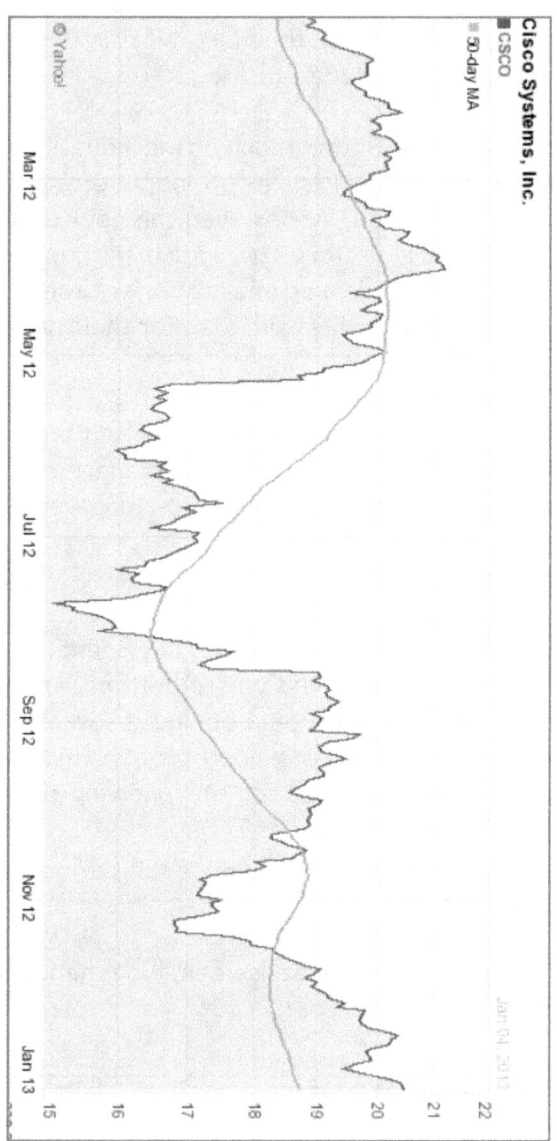

Table: CSCO 50-day SMA   Source: Yahoo!Finance

We can improve the trades by:
- Use different moving average in number of days (50 in this example) and other indicators such as EMA (a moving average that weighs higher

on more recent data). It may improve prediction accuracy and/or cut down the number of trades. RSI(14) suggests overbought / oversold conditions.

- Instead of selling the stock for cash, consider selling the stock short. Selling short is not for beginners for sure.

- The accuracy is usually improved by a separate chart for the sector the stock belongs to and another one for the market. For CSCO, you can use an ETF for network companies and SPY (or a similar ETF) to represent the market.

  In theory and in theory only, when both the stock, the sector that the stock is in and the market all move down, it has a high chance to move down, and vice versa.

  We use 50 days (in SMA) for short-term holding of stocks (90 days for longer holding), 90 days for the sector ETF and 350 days for SPY. Again, 'days' is actually 'trade sessions'.

TA is not for most fundamentalists but it should be used

For a bargain hunter like me, TA would not benefit me a lot for picking stocks at the bottoms. I would try to pick up CSCO with prices ranging from 15-17 and all below the moving average line that TA would not show me a Buy signal. However, for short-term swing traders TA is a Godsend.

To me, TA is good indicator for growth and momentum for short-term trading. Some fundamentalists may use TA for entry and exit point. Some recommend buying the stock when the price is above the SMA-200 (same as SMA-200% is positive that can be readily obtained from Finviz.com).

It is profitable for 'Buy High and Sell Higher' if you can protect your profits effectively. This is also called 'Buy at a reasonable cost'. One's opinion.

In selecting a tool, you have to understand how, why to use it and whether it fits your investing style. I use TA for market timing for the entire market more than on individual stocks. When I have more time, I would use TA more frequently. My portfolio has too many stocks that I should cut down.

Most of us cannot spot the bottom of a stock; I had some successes but most likely they were due to luck. When a stock is moving up from the bottom, there is a good chance it will move further up. TA shows it and its volume confirms it.

Conclusion

Even a fundamentalist like me can benefit a lot by using TA. This book touches the very basics of TA but the most useful TA indicators.

Besides monitoring the fundamentals of the stocks you bought once every 6 months, you should analyze their technical more often (1 month to 3 months depending on your available time). When the market is risky (close to the SMA average), run the SMA chart more frequently (say once a week).

Related topics:

Easy TA without charts

Bring up Finviz.com from your browser. Enter the stock you're evaluating. SMA-200% stands for Simple Moving Average of the last 200 trade sessions. RSI(14) is the relative strength index for the last 14 trade sessions.

The following is just a suggestion with conservative parameters. Adjust the parameters according to your risk tolerance and requirements. Do not buy the stock with SMA-200% is < 0 (trending down), SMA-200% > 40 (peaking), or RSI(14) > 55 (overbought).

Bollinger Bands

Bollinger Bands has been proven useful for traders. In theory, the stock is traded between the upper band and the lower band forming an envelope. For more info, click the following link.

http://www.investopedia.com/terms/b/bollingerbands.asp

The following chart was drawn by Yahoo!Finance for CSCO from 8/7/2012 to 8/7/2014 (today) selecting Bollinger Bands for the 50 days as a parameter. If you trade more often, use 20 days. If the chart is too small to display on your screen, enter the following in your PC's browser.

http://ebmyth.blogspot.com/2014/08/screen-csco-bollinger-bands-50.html

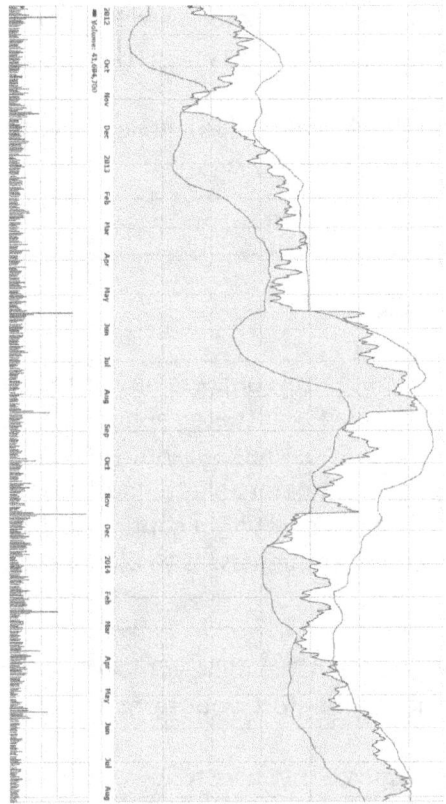

Bollinger Bands 50 Days.   Source: Yahoo!Finance

You buy the stock when the price is close to the lower band and sell the stock when it is close to the upper band.

When the stock price passes the upper band, it is called a breakout. Similar for the stock falling below the lower band.

From the above, we should make some good money but lose some opportunities as it did break out.

It is advisable to use at least one more technical indicator. I recommend RSI(14), which is also accessible from Yahoo!Finance or similar sites. When it is above 70, it is overbought, so I recommend selling the stock. When it is below 30, it is oversold, so I recommend buying the stock.

MACD

MACD, Moving Average Convergence Divergence, is an effective momentum (i.e. short-term) indicator used by most traders. When the stock price is crossing above the zero line, it is a buy and vice versa.

Again, try to master SMA and RSI(14) first. Using too many indicators usually harm you more than help you.

Filler:

A joke

I got an email from my potential congressman as follows:
The Supreme Court has ruled that there cannot be a Nativity Scene in the United States' Capital this Christmas Season. This isn't for any religious reason. They simply have not been able to find Three Wise Men in the Nation's Capital. The Search for a Virgin continues. There was no problem, however, finding enough asses to fill the stable.

My reply:
Beg to differ. All congressmen including yourself are wise men if you compare your bank account before your term and after.

You can find a lot of virgins but you've to lower your age requirement or change the definition of a virgin. For definition, borrow the example from Clinton's no smoker policy: As long as you do not exhale, you're a non-smoker. Change the word 'exhale' with many words I can think of but they are not too polite to write them down here - just in case the naive Sister Teresa is reading my blog secretly.

It appears to be a fact that there are more mouths kissing asses than asses available to be kissed. Hence, we really have a shortage of asses.

12   Monitor your traded stocks

After you have bought (or shorted) a stock, you need to monitor the progress and any new information about the stock.

First, you need to place stop orders to protect your portfolio unless you want to hold it forever. When the stock is rising, you may want to place trailing stops and review them periodically. You can check out the performances from your broker's statement (on-line preferred).

Second, you need to read as many articles about the stock. If you have a handful of stocks, Finviz is all you need. If you have a lot of stocks, I recommend some websites such as SeekingAlpha and MarketWatch to store your portfolio. Most have basic features and some have some features that are important to you. The following is a list of features you may consider.

- Let you create and delete watch lists. You may want to delete watch lists that you no longer need. Let you add / delete stocks in the watch list.

- Let you create multiple watch lists. You may have one for long-term holding (usually value stocks) and one for short-term holding (usually momentum stocks).

- Let you select the stock and display a list of articles related to that stock.

- Categorize the stocks by sectors. Unless you have a reason, you may want to diversify your portfolio such as not putting 50% of your portfolio in one sector.

- The performances of the stocks (from the date the stock is entered) and the performance of the watch list. The number of days held is useful to figure out the long-term or short-term capital gain/loss for non-retirement accounts.

Section III: Other strategies

1   Refined Dogs of Dow

What is it

Dogs of Dow is quite popular and even some mutual fund managers are using it exclusively. In a nutshell, you buy the ten Dow stocks that pay the highest dividend rates at year end and repeat the process every year. Ignore the stocks whose dividends are returns of capital. Click the above hyperlink for more info on this strategy.

(http://en.wikipedia.org/wiki/The_Dogs_of_the_Dow)

Past Performance

As of 2012, it just beats Dow and S&P 500 by a small margin in last decade except the last two years that are doing quite well.

The better performance of this strategy over the last two years could be due to the recent mild bubble on dividend growth stocks and most of those dogs belong to this group. Hence, be alert to when the dividend bubble bursts.

From Wikipedia,

"In fact, the Dogs of the Dow and Small Dogs of the Dow struggled to keep up with the Dow during latter stages of the dot-com boom (1998 and 1999) as well as during the financial crisis (2007-2009)."

My suggestion to improve the performance

1. Avoid stocks with high expected P/Es (i.e. > 40) such as most dot-com stocks in 2000.

2. Avoid sectors such as banks in 2007. Check the chapter "Sectors to be Cautious".

3. Practice market timing. Do not buy most stocks during market plunges and move back to equities in Early Recovery, a phase of the market cycle defined by me.

Improve the performance by customizing

When a strategy becomes popular, it will not perform due to the herd mentality (http://tonyp4idea.blogspot.com/2011/12/fool-of-all-fools.html).

Customize the strategy so that I do not pick the identical stocks as others who use the identical strategy.

Instead of buying the ten dogs, buy the first five dogs sorted by the forward (same as expected) positive P/E in ascending order (i.e. ignoring stocks with negative earnings).

This variation has an average annualized return of 15% (12% appreciation + estimated 3% dividend) from Nov. 1, 2000 to Nov. 1, 2010 from my testing. It is better than the original strategy already. The testing is for educational purpose only.

Another variation is: Buy the top five candidates on Nov. 1 and sell them on May 1 next year to benefit from the statistically favorable period.

Further Refining Dogs of Dow

The following are the variations to the original Dogs of Dow. Try out different combinations.

1. Include the stocks in S&P 500 and NASDAQ, so there are more stocks to choose from than just from the DOW.

2. Adjust the time between Dec. 1 and Dec. 15 (a little earlier is fine) instead of the start of the year to avoid the herd who follows the same strategy and performs the same task at the beginning of the year.

3. For retirement accounts or offsetting the short-term losers, try to buy on Nov.1 and sell on May 1 to take advantage of this normally favorable period.

4. Sort the selected top 10 with positive earnings by P/E in ascending order and buy the top 5. A value play. I prefer to skip P/E less than 4 as there may be something wrong with the company.

5. Avoid stocks in the following sectors: lenders, drug companies, miners, insurers and emerging.

6. Skip the companies that have serious lawsuits against them. Minor lawsuits are fine.

7. Avoid stocks that are being shorted in the range of 10% to 20%. The short % is defined by: No. of shares being shorted/Total floating shares. Stocks with short percent over 30% could trigger a short squeeze that could have great appreciation potential.

8. Use stop loss when the market is at the peak phase of the market cycle. For a better understanding of this, read the chapters on market timing.

9. Do not buy on the first year after the market plunge.

It is a lazy man's stock picking and market timing. I hope it performs better than the original strategy.

Afterthoughts

*

When you test out the above strategy, try different parameters. If possible, use the most recent data (such as the last ten years) to check out whether your strategy still works. If you are less risk tolerant, select the screened stocks with P/E between 4 and 12 only.

The following are some of the variance and can be combined into this strategy.

- Holding periods. Try 6 months, 11 months and 12 months.
- Buy contra ETFs during the unfavorable stock period such as May 1 to Nov. 1.
- Automatic your testing as much as possible, so you can add other parameters such as different holding periods.
- Avoid data fitting to obtain better results.

- Test for each stage of the market cycle.

*

Annualize the return if it is not 12 months for easier to compare. Do not get too excited on great returns. When you implement your strategy with real money, expect to beat the market by a small percentage only.

Review your test procedures when the return is excessive such as 60%. However, when you find one strategy yielding 60% and another one yielding 20% with same testing conditions, stick with the winner for real money.

Start with paper trading and then with a small portfolio.

There is no Holy Grail in investing. The market changes and it is not rational all the time otherwise there would be no poor folks. Investing with a good and proven strategy is better than investing without one.

*

Tom said:
Like every trading strategy, when everyone starts practicing it, the "advantage" goes away. We saw that plain and clear in 2008-09. Since nearly all financial advisors practice this discipline, it is no surprise to me that all correlations are slowly drifting to "1", and will probably stay that way until MPT losses steam.

[Tony: That's why I modified the original Dogs of Dow. I believe mine performs better and at less risk. As in any strategy, there is no guarantee.]

2 Tom's conservative strategy

The following is a summary of Tom's conservative strategy as described in his profile in Seeking Alpha website. Use it as an example and modify it to fit your investing philosophy. You need to ignore your friends telling you how much money he is making when the market is up. You also need not to tell them how much money you're not losing otherwise you do not have any friend.

I believe the best performance is achieved matching a strategy to the current market conditions and there is no Holy Grail in investing.

Click here for Tom's strategy.
(http://tonyp4idea.blogspot.com/2012/05/tom-armisteads-investment-strategy.html)

A winning strategy for couch potatoes

My friend Tom (no relationship) has a very similar strategy similar to Tom's. My friend is making money with the least risk. He only buys stocks after the market crashes and sell stocks when the market rises. Ignore all market pundits. It is recommended to anyone who does not have time to monitor his/her investment.

Enhance a good strategy.
Following the favorable stages to trade in the market cycle described in this book, buy in the Early Recovery phase (about 1 ½ year after the crash or use the entry point described in the chapters on Market Timing), sell in one or two years after and maintain cash for the rest of the time.

Optionally add a small amount of purchases in Nov. 1 and sell them in April 1. Optionally buy in Dec. 1 and sell in Feb. 1 to take advantage of the best (statistically) period of the year. Add long term bonds when the interest rates is high (say more than 5%) and you do not have to sell these bonds.

Spend the rest of the time in the comfortable couch (i.e. enjoying life) or sip some fancy tropical drink served by some beautiful tropical lady in some nice tropical island. Not a bad strategy!

Top down approach

1. Is it a good time to buy stocks (via market timing)?
2. What sectors to buy?
3. Screen out about 10 stocks in that sector.
4. Further evaluate each stock.
5. Optionally, use Technical Analysis to see the best time and price to buy the selected stocks.
6. Periodically monitor your stocks. Sell some if necessary and go to Step 1.

When you buy at the bottom, buy value stocks only.

The easiest retirement planning system

Have a budget and live within your means. Buy good stuff that last for a long time. After saving enough cash for emergency and planned expenses such as vacation, new car, college, etc., invest your extra money in a retirement account (Roth IRA if allowable) with 80% in a market ETF and 20% in a short-term bond ETF.

Run the chart described in the market cycle chapters once a month. If the chart tells you to exit the market, move all to cash. Reenter the market when the chart tells you so. It beats most if not all of your financial plans from the best experts money can buy.

Afterthoughts

My late friend had a 'buy and hold strategy' that worked pretty well. Most of his stocks were big companies. He died with a house worth more than a million and many millions in stocks. His only mistake was not to transfer more of his stocks to his heirs before his death. He died on the year when the estate exemption returned back to a million. Uncle Sam was the biggest winner and won big without any effort.

3 The best strategy

Buy Low and Sell High.

It is simple but most retail investors just do the opposite: Buy High and Sell Low. The flow of money to/from money market funds turns out to be a reliable contrary indicator.

2003, 2009 and the later part of June, 2012 could be the best time to buy.

The above represents buy at low prices and sell at high prices. Considering P/E (positive 'E' only), buy at low P/E of a stock, a sector and the market and sell them respectively at high P/E.

Here are some hints when to buy and sell with this strategy:

- Sell when everyone including your silly mother-in-law is making good money and all think they're market geniuses. It could be the riskiest time. The high interest rates usually confirms this as folks falsely expect better return even they pay more to borrow money to buy stocks.

- Do not buy the stocks that were the bubble stocks such as the technology stocks in 2001-2002 and the bank stocks in 2008-2009 as some 'optimists' think it is time to return and usually they're wrong.

  Do not think the stock is a good deal when it loses half of its value. Buy them only when the root problem has been fixed. The best time to return to the market after a market plunge is usually two years after the market plunge (2003 for the market plunge in 2000 and 2009 for the market plunge in 2007). Many bubble stocks never recover and many of these stocks take more than 2 years to recover. Their prices appear to be low, but not low enough. Some bubble stock can go to zero.

- Be careful on the sector or group of stocks that have winning streak for more than two years. Most likely they will correct. Use stop loss to protect your profits if you want to keep them.

  You could have saved a lot if you use this strategy on tech stocks in 2000. As of 2014, dividend stocks could be the next sector to burst but only time can tell. Do not fall in love with a stock. Yesterday's winners could be tomorrow's losers, and vice versa. If you do not want to sell your big winners now, at least protect your profits.

'Buy and hold' is dead since 2000. We have two market plunges with an average loss of over 45% from their highs.

- Do not buy dividend stocks solely for dividends. They usually lose less value in a recession after dividends, but they will not make a lot when the recession is over. In addition, consider any changes in tax laws that may not be favorable for dividends.

    As of 2013 and depending on your tax situations, your dividend tax could be as high as 20% and your highest income tax rate could be close to 40%. Hence, when you withdraw from your retirement accounts except from Roth accounts, it will be treated as income which could double your tax from dividends. It is a myth of paying no tax on dividends on retirement accounts unless it is a Roth IRA or your retirement income is low.

- Buy value stocks that seem to be bottomed. It is hard to identify the bottom. When the potential profit outweighs the risk, it is a buy.

    As of 6/2013, coal stocks may have been bottomed out. Oil and other resource stocks could have been bottomed out too. As of 2012, health care should be bottomed out judging from their low P/Es. All these industrial commodities will not truly recover until the global economy recovers.

- Buy the stocks that have been losing money but their burn rates can last for the entire recession. They're risky but the potential profits are great. We can find many in 2003 and 2009. Today as of 2012, P/Es of a few corporations are at historical low even in a bad economy.

- Buy against the experts who have unconvincing predictions. They usually exaggerate the rosy outlooks of the companies in order to sell the stocks they own. This is one of the few times you should bet against them. Use your better judgment to ensure how false their predictions would be.

- No one can predict consistently when the market is bottom. However, use your better judgment with educated guesses to gain an edge. Refer to the exit point using the 350-day SMA from the chapter on detecting market plunges.

Using Citicorp (symbol C) as an example

Following the chapter on avoiding bank stocks, buying this stock at $550 a share could be avoided. After the big plunge (2008), I believe it has long-term profit potential. Accumulate this stock if you believe C will be profitable in 10 years (2024) or so. Do not sell it unless there is potential for a market plunge. If so, buy it back after the plunge. One's opinion.

With our market timing, we should come back to the 2 years after the start of the market plunge. Optionally we use the SMA-350 to determine the reentry point. However, it has no meaning due to the big plunge from $550. On 8/2009, C's P/E was negative, so it was still not bought.

Buy it for every big drop in P/E as follows. We started when the P/E is about 40. Normally I buy at around 20. Take an exception for turnaround stocks.

Date	P/E	Price
06/2010	40	40
01/2011	13	49
08/2011	9	32

The above is for illustration only, so the numbers are not precise.

As of 6/12/2014, I expect a correction, so we may want to sell some at about $48. Today, this portfolio of the 3 buys is about breaking even and not beating the SPY (the market to most). However, long-term profit potential is great. The other three important metrics are P/B, P/S and RSI(14). Use forward (expected) P/E if possible.

The second best strategy

Buy high and sell higher.

When everyone is looking for stocks with the highest value, there may not be any such stocks available. It seems to contradict with my best strategy but it is not. Fundamentals may not show everything about the company such as a new drug, a new product... The all-time high prices usually show that. Buy the stock when it is over the 50-day simple moving average (50 or 200 days depending on how long you usually hold a stock).

Buying fully-priced stocks is dangerous even it is profitable. To protect your profits:

- Be extra careful in risky market; I prefer not to buy any stock when the market is risky.

- Set stop loss orders. Recommend 10% (or 15% for volatile stocks) less than the current price. If you set 5% stop, it would be stopped out for normal fluctuations.

- Use Technical Analysis. When the price drops below the moving average you used, sell it. When RSI (14) is high (over 70), check out the reason as it could be overbought.

If you are not very sure, sell half of it. You will not get broke for taking profits.

As in life, there are no guarantees, but using a proven technique / discipline is far better than trading without one. Paper trading to ensure the strategy fits the current market conditions and your personal tolerance and requirements.

The third best strategy

Buy high and sell even higher.

It is the riskiest. These stocks could be bubble stocks moved by institution investors and then moved higher by retail investors. It may take a while before the institution investors rotate to another sectors / stocks.

My strategy is to follow the herd but ensure you're ready to exit.

- Identify them. Usually they are large caps with high trade volumes.

- Do not short them.

- Buy them ignoring the fundamentals. Alternatively, use options.

- Set stop losses for stocks and ETFs. Adjust the stops periodically after they appreciate.

    Watch it every day. Bring up Finviz.com and enter the sector ETF the stock belongs or the stock itself. Pay attention to SMA200%: The higher it is, the higher chance it is peaking. When RSI(14) is over 70% (65% for sectors), most likely it is overbought.

Picture filler:

Section IV: Trading stocks

1   Order prices

Market orders

Use market orders only when it is necessary (more later) as stocks price can easily be manipulated especially on stocks with low trading volumes.

However, in a rising market, many fast rising stocks can only be bought via market orders. Many winners never take a breather on their way up.

In my momentum portfolio on 11/2013, I placed a sell price for GERN far higher than the market price. Surprisingly I sold it for this price making an annualized return of 1,176% for holding it for 21 days. When there are few or no other sellers for the stock, the market price would be the price you set. If I cannot sell it in the next 9 days (30 days is my holding period for momentum stocks), I would set it lower. Update: One year later, GERN lost 29%.

Sensible discounts

I prefer to buy the stock at the price closest to the last trade price (to most it is the market price). I seldom lose buying these orders. Sometimes I use the day's lowest price to buy (or the highest to sell) plus a penny (or minus a penny for sell prices to sell).

My other purchase strategy is using 0.15% or 0.25% less than the current prices for stocks I really want. For some promising stocks, I buy them at almost the market price and then place another order on the same stock at 0.5% less than the last traded price (and sometimes 2% depending on the current market trend).

We all want to buy less and sell at higher prices. However, if the trade price is too far away from the current market price (such as 5% from the market price), these trades may never be executed. I have had a long list of buy orders that were not executed and turned out to be big gainers. Learn from my bad experiences.

Use a good discount (such as 10% from the market price) if you believe the market, the sector or the stock will dip by 10%. After you bought the stock, you place a sell order 10% more than the price you paid for it hoping the stock will return to the original price and you pocket 10%. Wishful thinking! However, it has happened to me several times primarily due to temporary market dips.

It works when there is a correction and/or the stock is very volatile. It is usually within the 5% range to take advantage of these situations, not the 10% as described. For a 10% plunge, it usually is due to some serious problem of the company surfacing. One common reason is not meeting its earnings expectation and in this case it usually continues its downward trend.

Larger discounts on a falling market

During a falling market (or a mild correction), 3% less than the current prices for buy orders may be fine for some stocks (use 5% for volatile stocks). To illustrate, I placed about 10 of these orders over the last two months during a market dip. Most of the orders were filled. When the market is plunging, do not buy any stock.

Caterpillar and Cisco were some of my buys at these discounts. They were in my watch list to buy. Initially these shares often fall even lower as the trend was downward. As of 12/18/12, CAT earned me from 3% and 14% (bought in 6/12 and 7/12) and CSCO bought in 7/14/12 returned about 34%. My original objective: Buy deeply-valued stocks, wait and sell them when the economy returns.

When you predict the market will dip by 5%, set your buy orders accordingly. Again, predictions are just educated guesses. From my experience, they work most of the time but not all of the time.

On the day of the earnings announcement, the fluctuation of the stock is usually high. Check any change in the earnings estimate before the announcement and act accordingly. Zacks is supposed to be a useful tool to predict earnings estimates. Do not leave orders during the earnings announcement dates, which can be found on Finviz. When the earning turns out to be good, the stock price surges and your order will not be executed. When the earnings are bad, the stock price will plunge usually and you most likely overpaid.

Option expiration dates usually cause more volatility. Retail investors do not have to be concerned except you may use wider stops. In theory, dividend days have little effect on the stock price as it will be lowered by the dividend amount.

High volume of a stock could mean opportunity

High volume usually increases the stock price volatility. If the volatility of a stock increases substantially (such as doubling its average daily volume), there could be important news on the company, recommendation changes from a major analyst or trading by the institutional investors. It usually takes the institutional investors a week to trade a stock with their sizable positions.

Many times it is started by the insiders who know about the breaking news of a stock before it is publicized. Some investment services / sites specialize in identifying the increasing volumes on these stocks.

Because day traders do not want to leave any open positions overnight, higher volatility occurs at the end of the day. It is the same on the day (usually on Friday) when the options are expiring.

Monitor your trade prices

You cannot tell whether you are paying a fair price without keeping a record. To illustrate, you're paying 1% less than the market prices in buying stocks. You may have missed buying some winners. If the 1% you saved is smaller than the appreciation of the stocks you would have bought at market prices, then you should adjust the buy prices to 0.5% less than the market price and monitor again.

Market trend makes a difference too. When the market is trending up, buying any stock would most likely be profitable and usually the purchase orders with higher discounts will not be executed.

Follow the same logic on sell orders. Need to have at least 25 stock purchases (and potential purchases) to make the conclusion meaningful. If you do not trade a lot, you will not have enough data to verify. As described, I prefer not to place an order during the earnings announcement dates which can be found on Finviz.com. If you cannot buy the stock, consider to use market order the next day.

Good prospects

When you find gems especially those stocks that are followed by analysts, buy them at market prices and consider doubling the bet if you are really sure you have a winner. From my super stock screens, I spotted NHTC. I placed several bets and one market order. All of them were NOT executed except with the market order. At the end of the day NHTC is up 18% and my executed order is up 14%. I did not have the best buy but made a good profit. NHTC was on its way to a huge appreciation and I sold it too early. I have earned not to sell a winner and protect the profit with a stop.

Lower the buy for risky stocks (if the beta from Finviz is greater than 1 for example) even if they have good fundamentals.

Quality over quantity

If your time is limited, spend all the time on researching one stock one at a time. However, you need to own at least 3 stocks (more stocks for a large portfolio) for your diversification purposes.

Double your normal purchase position on stocks that look great after the research. For risky stocks that look good, you may want to halve your normal purchase position to cut down on the risk. If you are less risk tolerant, do not buy risky stocks at all. My results are not conclusive on risky stocks but I do get a good sleep.

A recent example
Recently I sold EA with $1 more than my order price but $2 less than the current price of the day, which was the earnings announcement day. I do recommend not placing orders right before the earnings announcement day for the stock. If the earnings are good, you do not get all the profit as in this real example; my broker did get me $1 more. If the earnings are bad, you will not sell it any way. It is the same for buying stocks.

2   Stop loss & flash crash

You can limit your stock loss with stops. There are some incidents where you do not always want to use a stop loss.

- <u>Flash crash</u> (May 6, 2010 also August 2015).
  It would turn your stops into market orders that could be substantially lower than your stop prices. Some brokers offer stop limits, but they do not guarantee the orders will be executed.

  The better way is a "mental stop" (my term). You do not place a stop order but place a market order to sell when your stock falls below a pre-defined price. During flash crashes, you do not want to place the market orders to sell but place orders to buy from your watch list.

  I bought some stocks at more than 10% discount during the flash crash (actually I could buy them even at better discounts) and within a week most had returned to the prices as before the flash crash.

  Placing buy orders with huge discounts to the market prices works better for volatile stocks. You should cancel the unexecuted trades before the weekends / holidays and reenter them afterwards to avoid unexpected events that may affect the stock prices.

  Avoid trading drug and bio tech companies with huge differences to the market prices. High tech is a good sector for this purpose and fluctuating 10% in this sector is more of a norm than an exception. Buying an ETF at 5% discount is a better bet than buying specific stocks from my experience.

- My experience with 911.
  I sold many stocks due to stop orders during 911. The market came back in the next three days and I missed the recovery from the stocks that were sold and did not buy back them in time.

- If your stocks are rising, you need to adjust the stop loss prices accordingly. To illustrate- in maintaining a 10% stop loss, your stop is at 90 when the current price is 100. When the stock price rises to 200, it should be adjusted to $180 (10% less than the current price). It is also called a trailing stop.

Most brokers allow you to enter most trades "Good till Cancelled". Even for that there is an expiration date such as 6 months for Fidelity. Fidelity's trades for Short Sell expire by the end of the trade session. Check your broker's current policy.

- Risky markets.
  When the market is risky, you may want to use a stop loss. To prevent another flash crash, you may want to use a 'mental' market order. It is not perfect, as it requires constant watching of the market.

  There are many investing services and sites that give you the 'right' prices for a stop loss. Basically it depends on how volatile are the specific stocks. The chartists will tell you under normal conditions stocks are trading between the resistance line and the support line. Use the stop loss just below the resistance line to avoid the stop order from being executed due to the volatility of the stock.

  For simplicity as I have too many stocks in my portfolio, I use a percent. In the old days, it was recommended 8% or so below the prices you paid. In today's volatile market, I recommend 12%.

- Risky stocks.
  A stop loss is the only way that you can limit your loss for big drop (such as 25%). Affimax lost 85% of its stock value in one day with the news that three of its patients died.

- Low-volume stocks.
  The market order could drive the prices right down as there are few buyers in low-volume stocks. If there is only one buyer, he will buy with the best price for him (or the worst price to the seller).

  Unless I have good reasons, I would skip the low-volume stocks. I define low-volume: If my buy amount is higher than 1% of the average daily amount (= average daily volume * stock price).

- Beta.
  Stocks may be more volatile than the market. Beta is used to measure its volatility. The market can be measured by the S&P 500 index. If the beta of a stock is 1, its volatility is the same as the market. If it is 1.2, it is 20% more volatile.

Set a lower stop loss for volatile stocks to prevent stocks from selling due to regular fluctuations.

Afterthoughts

Let me show you my bitter experience. The following are 5 stocks I wanted to buy and the average return was quite good.

Stocks	Return
URI	63%
GMCR	572%
MTW	186%
PII	-74%
TSCO	-127%
Avg.	124%

I placed buy orders at 5% less than the market prices as most 'bargain' investors do. I bought both of the two losers but no winners. The winners never took a breather on its way up, but the losers went down. I did buy GMCR via a market order in my momentum strategy in a separate account.

#Filler: Rocket stocks

As of 6/2017, TSLA, AMAZ, NFLX and AAPL were all overpriced by most fundamental metrics. However, they are the darlings of institutional investors. My advice is not to do anything (not to buy and not to short them) as we cannot fight the city hall and their momentum.

3   Short selling

You sell short a stock because you believe it is going down in price. It could be used to hedge the downside of a related stock you own. Shorting should be avoided for beginner investors.

Advantages

You believe the stock and or the market (using contra ETFs that represent the market) is going down.

What to buy & how

If Fidelity's Equity Summary Score for the stock is below 4, it is a short candidate.

The following are my suggestions on shorting stocks that have the potential to go down. Basically these stocks are both fundamentally unsound and technically unsound. Many sites (some require paid subscriptions) provide a composite grade for fundamentals and technical. Finviz.com does provide most of these metrics and many are used in the following discussion. If you combine the following metrics, then most likely you may need to compromise on some metrics to make your decision to short or not.

- Fundamentals

  - The price is more than four times the book value.
  - EY is negative. Negative PEG is another consideration.
  - High debts (Debt/Equity > .5) except for industries that require high debts.
  - Insiders are unloading their company's stocks. They do this for many reasons. But, when they are buying, do not short the stock as they may know some positive events we do not know.
  - Bad intangibles such as losing market share and/or a major lawsuit(s) is pending.
  - Read articles on the company from Finviz, Fidelity, Seeking Alpha, etc.
  - Do not short stocks that are on their uptrend. It includes the current marijuana stocks that most have no fundamental values and/or historical data.

- Do not short small stocks with a small market cap or float. I usually short stocks with a market cap or float > 200M. Use higher values for conservative investors.

  The stocks with small floats may be controlled by the owners – if they do not sell, the stocks available to trade will be limited. Another indicator is the Avg. Daily Vol.

- Technical metrics:

  - Do not short when the stock plunged more than 10% recently. It could mean the bottom has been reached.
  - Overbought (RSI(14) > 60). There may be a reason, so it is only a secondary consideration. Most stocks to be shorted may have RSI(14) < 30.
  - The momentum metrics such as SMA-20 and SMA-50 are important too. SMA-20% from Finviz.com should be negative.
  - Some sites especially the paid sites may give you a momentum grade. Select the stocks with a bad momentum grade (a.k.a. timing grade) but not the worst grade (as it has nowhere to go but up).

- Trading considerations

  - Do not trade in the first hour (first half hour for me) as there may have new developments overnight.
  - Your short trade (limited order) may only be valid for the day; check this with your broker. It is good for your trade too. For example, I placed a short sell order for MRSN and it was cancelled at the end of the day. The next day it was up by 16%.
  - Your broker may need to approve whether you can short stocks.
  - When you sell short and are using limit orders, enter a sell price higher than the last trade price just like selling a stock.
  - Close the short position when your trade loses a pre-defined percentage which depends on your personal tolerance.

Disadvantages and some suggestions

- Short stocks when the market is plunging and limit your shorting positions when the market is rising.

- Could lose more than 100% of the investment.

Actually, in theory, there is no limit. If the shorted stock price rises by 10 times, the loss is well over 10 times the money invested. The 2015 example was Weight Watchers. The price boosted up by more than 170% when Oprah took out a position on them. Fundamentally this stock was not sound and it should be shorted. No stock pickers can predict that. Use mental stops to protect your trade.

- Need to pay dividends and interest for the shorted stock.
  The higher the dividend rate for the stock, the more you have to pay. Experienced investors should avoid high-dividend stocks when shorting unless the expected shorting period is only brief.

  In addition, you need to pay interest for 'borrowing' the stocks to sell. Brokers charge interest rates differently and it could be huge savings to shop around if you short stocks a lot.

- Need both fundamental and technical analyses.
  From my experience, technical analysis is more important than fundamentals in shorting.

- If shorting a stock is successful and closed within a year, the gain is usually subjected to the short-term capital gains taxes which are typically higher than the long-term capital gains taxes. Check current tax laws.

- Not all of the stocks can be shorted. Your broker may not have the stock you want to short. It is also possible that your broker can close out your short positions for various reasons. Check the margin status with your broker.

- Selling short is not allowed in retirement accounts as of 2016. However, you can buy contra ETFs for a group of stocks to bet against the market or a specific sector, but not on a specific stock in retirement accounts.

- The following sectors are riskier: the drug, mine, bank (unless you know the quality of their mortgages) and insurance sectors. An approval of a drug could drive the stock price up by more than 25% in one day. The same for earnings announcements. It could drive the stock more than 25% in either direction.

- Your screens may find many stocks in bio tech companies. These companies especially with a market cap of less than 1B have the worst fundamentals. However, when they have a new discovery, the stock prices could rocket. Do not short them when insiders are buying (Insider Transaction on Finviz.com) and high SMA-20% (from Finviz.com).

- There is no perfect timing. Some stocks fluctuate a lot with no rational reasons, or the prices are driven by institutional investors. Some stocks could be manipulated. The shorted stocks could move up for a long time until they finally crash.

- A bad company could be acquired by another company due to a good buy; it could boost its stock price.

- Use mental stops (i.e. set a price you can afford to lose and when it reaches the specific price, place a market trade to exit the shorted shares. You do not want to make 5% several times and lose 50% in one trade.

- You may not want to short companies that are fundamentally unsound with a good momentum. They may have good prospects such as improved profit, being turned around, settling a lawsuit and/ or new products are being legalized and/or approved. If you do, then use mental stops to protect your trades.

- Watch out for short squeezes when the short percentage approaches over 25%. In a nut shell, the stock is running out of shares to be shorted. As a result, it would rise in price especially on any good news. As of 8/2015, I expect short squeeze for PPC and SAFM (CALM in 12/2015) for the following reasons:

    1. The shorting has no bases. It is most likely from one or two hedge funds.
    2. Fundamentally sound.
    3. Beef will be replaced by a lot of healthier and cheaper chicken if not already, esp. during the drought in California.
    4. In Hong Kong for example, they do not allow live chickens imported from China during the bird flu breakout, but they did allow frozen chicken from the USA if there was no political game going on.

Put Option
It is similar to shorting a company with more advantages than disadvantages. It is not for beginners.

Margin

Margin should not be used extensively. It is expensive and most brokers try every trick they can to squeeze profits from all transactions to subsidize their low-commission incomes. Usually you can borrow up to 40% of your current position and the rules and the margin rates vary among brokers.

Many investors had losses during the last two market plunges. However, many including myself had made a killing in 2003 and 2009 using margin. I use it for the following reasons.

- For convenience in placing buy orders that exceed my cash position in my taxable accounts.

- I can pay back my outstanding margin loans from my home equity loan (check the current tax laws) as it is far, far lower than my broker's margin interest rates. However, I do not recommend this for conservative investors.

Links & Articles
Tilson
Put Options.http://en.wikipedia.org/wiki/Put_option
Fidelity Video: Options.https://www.fidelity.com/learning-center/options/finding-options-strategies/options-analysis-tool-video
Fidelity Video: Selling short.https://www.fidelity.com/learning-center/trading/selling-short-video

4   Covered calls

For basic descriptions on a covered call from Wikipedia, click [here](http://en.wikipedia.org/wiki/Covered_call) or enter (http://en.wikipedia.org/wiki/Covered_call) in your browser.

It is like collecting rent from the apartment you bought. The difference is that the renter has an option to buy the apartment at a preset time and price.

The rent is quite substantial if you do good planning. To start with, you want to buy stocks that have a market to sell. Usually they are large companies with high trading volumes.

Since one contract is for 100 shares of a stock, you cannot sell a covered call on 50 shares of a stock. On the other hand, when you have 1,000 stocks, the commission of 10 contracts would be more than the cost of 1 contract depending on your broker's schedule.

It is time consuming to keep track of the covered calls but it is well worth your time and effort. If the stock price exceeds the strike price of your covered call, you may want to buy the same shares back, so you would not miss any further appreciation of this stock.

However, if it is in a taxable account and you have a loss in a forced sell, do not buy it back otherwise the tax loss is not allowed (i.e. a wash sale) for the year as of 2016. When the contract expires, you may want to start another contract on the same stock if the stock has not been sold.

Covered calls do have their disadvantages such as higher commission rates and sometimes forcing you to sell at a higher tax rate for short-term capital gains in taxable accounts. It is avoidable by using covered calls on stocks that are qualified for long-term capital gains. In addition, you need to buy them back when they increase in price beyond your strike price or lose its potential to appreciate further. Using another put could keep you from not losing any gains beyond the strike price. However, I prefer to use my time in more productive ways and this insurance is not cheap. One's opinion.

One company advertises their techniques using covered calls which could give their users 3 to 6% monthly returns. If you believe in this fantasy, you do not need this book. There is no free lunch.

My recent experience

I sold Netflix covered calls with the strike price about 2% higher and a 3% premium (from my memory) but the price shot up 12% higher in one day, so I was potentially losing 7% profit. However, it turned out to be a good experience as Netflix went downhill later (8/2012).

Normally I prefer to sell covered options for stocks with a quantity from 100 to 600 shares (i.e. 1 to 6 contracts) for the longest time (about 2-3 months). Some non-volatile and small stocks are not candidates to write covered calls on. Some stocks are not optionable. Typically high-tech stocks have a higher premium to be collected as their stock prices fluctuate more. The right stocks can generate 10% or even more a year in addition to the fluctuations of the stock prices.

In general, if I feel the market will be down for the period, I use covered calls especially for stocks holding over one year (unless I have short-term loss to offset any short-term gains) in taxable accounts. Watch out for any tax change that may affect your total return.

Recently I attended a sales pitch on a 3-day training course on a strategy for making 24% per year and it is quite possible especially with the S&P 500 returns about the same. I wish it were available to me 15 years ago. It seems to be too good to be true.

How to sell covered calls

First you need to open an account with your broker and apply to trade options including covered calls.

Check how your broker charges commissions. Ask how much they charge for one contract and 10 contracts of a stock.

The covered call is an agreement to sell the rights to the buyer of the stock at the strike price for a specific date range (a.k.a. expiration date). Typically options expire on Fridays.

You need to write covered calls on the stocks you already own. One contract is 100 shares of stocks. Check out the option chain to select the price, expiration period and the strike price. Normally, the strike price should be higher than the current market price. You may want to have an expiration date 2 weeks or longer. When the contract is expiring in a few days, the contract has little value and most likely the small 'rent' is not worth the risk and the commission.

When the covered call is sold, you receive the 'rent' immediately and any dividend during the 'rental' period.

When the option is 'called' due to a price rise above the strike price, your stock will be sold and you will have to pay the regular commission.

At this point, evaluate the stock to check whether you want to buy it back. If the stock surges, you may have to pay a higher price – thus losing the extra appreciation. In addition, you may have to pay a higher capital gains tax if it is held less than the required period for long-term capital gains in a taxable account.

Note. Notice that some stocks are not optionable and/or not practical to write options on. Most brokers charge a flat rate for the first contract (such as $7) and an incremental fee for each additional contract. Shop around as the fees vary if you write a lot of covered calls.

The best stocks for covered calls are large US companies with a large average volume. The option (a.k.a. the 'rent') pays better for volatile companies such as high-tech companies. From my rough estimates for illustration purposes, the annualized return on covered calls for AAPL is 25% and C is 12% after commission.

5   Diversification

LTCM, a hedge fund run by smart people, and Isaac Newton both made one serious mistake about investing. They both bet all in one bet and they lost it big. They were the smartest folks on earth but they violated one basic principle about investing: diversification.

Another example is the potato. Irish made good living in their primary crop: potato. When a virus came, they lost all the potatoes and caused the potato famine.

Diversification improves a portfolio's performance in the long run and it reduces risk. Diversification includes other asset class besides stocks such as oil, gold, cash (yes even cash as a safety net to grasp better opportunities ahead), real estate, etc. However, stocks historically produce the best return. In addition, most stocks are quite liquid as it takes a minute to sell them compared to selling a house for example. You can buy other assets such as gold (GLD), money market funds and real estate (via REITs) via the low-cost ETFs.

When an asset is over-valued, it will return to the average historical value with one or two exceptions. Gold is one exception, but it is partly due to the depreciation of USD and the previous prolonged downfall of gold adjusted to inflation.

Simply put, owning 10 to 15 good stocks with less than three stocks in the same sector (which have to be good sectors to start with) achieves diversification goal for most. When one sector crashes, you still have two more good sectors.

Every one's situation is different:

- Depends on your wealth and your age.
  For younger folks with limited wealth (less than $50,000 to invest), a portfolio of 3 stocks (preferably most in ETFs) in different sectors or one diversified ETF could be enough. Your objective about investing is saving money for a down payment for a house, paying your loans including college loans and/or improving your earning power by taking classes.

Retirees may want to maintain a larger percentage of your holdings in cash and/or invested in bonds (long-term bonds could be very risky when the interest rates is going up). Those wealthy enough can fully invest in stocks as losing 50% of their portfolio doesn't alter their lifestyle. Most business owners should invest in stocks and other vehicles instead of plowing back to their businesses in order to diversify their investments.

Portfolios with more than a billion dollars such as in most mutual funds owning 10 stocks with 100 million each are just too risky to me.

Holding cash is safe but it loses its value due to inflation. To illustrate this point, consider these three scenarios in 1950:

1. An apartment bought in for $10,000 in NYC or in your home town.

2. An investment in the Dow Jones 30 Industrials for $10,000.

3. A 3.5% certificate of deposit or one of the U.S. Treasuries for your $10,000.

By now, all real estate investments should have appreciated many, many times over and most stock shares value would have multiplied also. The $10,000 CD gain has lost real value due to inflation. Our capitalist system punishes us for not taking risk. In the long term, risk is smoothed out over time.

- Excessive frequency in re-balancing your portfolio for diversification takes up time from evaluating stocks. It may cost you in transaction fees but they are low in today's self-directed brokerage accounts. In addition, it may have some tax consequences in taxable accounts.

  The advantage of churning the portfolio (but not excessively) can improve the quality of your portfolio with most updated information about the companies you invest in.

  Many brokers display your current diversification in your monthly statement summaries. If not, use a simple spreadsheet to classify the sectors and the asset classes in your portfolio.

- Diversification can easily be achieved by buying indexed funds and/or ETFs. They are less volatile. I recommend it to all folks with less than $50,000 to invest.
- Diversification does not mean to pick simply a stock in other sectors that has the opposite correlation from the stocks you own. The stock quality comes first.
- Diversification takes a back seat to spotting market plunges. When most stocks plunge such as during 2007-2008, diversification does not save your portfolio, but spotting and reacting to market plunges will.
- Some of our stocks will lose value. If they were due to our mistakes, write them down and learn from them. If they were frauds (not avoidable in many cases), diversification would limit our losses
- Over diversified is not too good either. With too many stocks you own, you may not have time to monitor them. Focus investing could be very profitable.

My suggestions on diversification

Portfolio up to	Strategy	For stock pickers
$ 50,000	ETF that simulates the market	5 stocks
$100,000	80% in ETF and 20% in a sector ETF(s)	10 stocks
$500,000	10 stocks with less than 3 in same sector.	15 stocks with less than 3 in same sector.
$1 Million	15 stocks + at least 20% in ETFs.	20 or more stocks depending on your time available and less than 4 in same sector.

As described, everyone's situation is different. If you have more time for investing, you should be able to handle more than 10 stocks. Playing market timing (i.e. switching to cash) depends on one's risk tolerance. If you are good at stock picking, you should buy stocks instead of ETFs. On a personal note, I usually have more than 10 stocks.

6   *When to sell a stock*

There are many reasons to sell a stock as follows.

Personal

1. Has met the targets/objectives.
   It could be 10% gain in a very short-term swing, x% return in 4 months for a short-term swing or y% gain after a year for long-term trades. Define x and y depending on your risk tolerance and how often you trade.

   I bought 4 stocks in one day during the August, 2015 correction and placed sell orders with 10% more than my purchase prices. I sold one in a day and another one within a month.

   Never look back and do not blame yourself when the prices are better than your trade prices. When the market is volatile, use a higher percent of the current prices. Be disciplined. Stay on the same strategy and detach yourself from emotions.

2. Realize that we have made a mistake. Do not let our ego blocking our eyes. It could be due to bad analysis, unexpected frauds, lawsuits, and/or bad data. It is better to get out with a small loss. I prefer 25% loss as a threshold. A trader may prefer 10% or even less.

   We have to ensure whether it is a mistake or not. If the 'mistake' is just bad luck or due to conditions we cannot possibly predict or control, then it is not a mistake. If it is a mistake, learn from it. When we diversify, one bad loss would not cause a big dent to our portfolios. Stop loss is a good tool most of the time except on flash crashes.

   If the criteria have been faithfully followed and it does not work well, check out whether your criteria are wrong or it does not work on the current market conditions.

3. When we have too many stocks in the same sector, we want to replace some stocks to diversify our portfolios.

When the sector is rising, we want to weigh more on the sector at the expense of diversification, and vice versa. Set a limit of how many sectors you are holding.

4. Need cash for living expenses.

5. To reduce tax burden by selling some losers. Tax consideration should not be the primary reason for selling. Take advantage of the favorable tax treatments of long-term capital gains. In short, sell losers within the short term and sell winners after 365 days; check current tax laws.

   Harvest tax losses. Sell losers and buy back similar stocks. It is not too clear that you can buy back the same loser in your children's account under the current tax law. Avoid wash sales that you cannot incur the tax loss for the same year.

6. To take advantage of low tax. In 2013, we can pay virtually zero (except the increase of tax on social security payment) Federal income tax on long-term capital gains when our income is below a specific tax bracket (15% as of 2015). Check the current tax laws. Evaluate the sold winners for possible buy back.

Market Timing

7. When the market or the sector plunges, sell stocks.

   For temporary peaks, do not sell all stocks, but those stocks whose fundamentals have been deteriorated more than the other stocks in your portfolio. The objective is to raise cash for buying opportunity.

Deteriorating appreciation potential

8. There may be some stocks that have better appreciation potential than the ones you currently own. Churning the portfolio by replacing better stocks may cost some brokerage commissions and taxes, but it improves the quality and appreciation potential for the entire portfolio.

9. The company's fundamentals have changed for the worse. If you use a scoring system, compare the current score with the score you bought

the stock. Apple is a good example from 2013 to 2015. Buy when the fundamentals are good and sell when they are not.

The common ones are expected P/E, the earnings growth rate and the sales growth rate.

When they have passed the peak and started to decline, sell them. When they are heading to bankruptcy, sell them fast.

Hints that the fundamentals are degrading

Evaluate the stocks you own at least every 6 months and check their daily news at least once a week (easily done using Seeking Alpha's portfolio function).

- The cash flow is decreasing fast. Cash flow is not a particularly good predictive indicator for appreciation, but a good indicator on whether the company will survive. This metric is very hard to be manipulated.

- A new or pending lawsuit. Check how serious is the lawsuit and minor lawsuits can be ignored.

- When the SEC pays attention to a company, it usually means bad news.

- Increasing receivable and/or inventory.

- Big drop in sales. Do not be alarmed when a new product or a new drug is going to replace a major product. Compare sales to the same quarter of prior year to avoid seasonal fluctuations (easily done using Finviz.com).

- Short percentage is increasing fast – someone found something wrong with the company.

- The invalidity of 'one-time charges'.

- Abnormal return rate of the company's pension fund comparing to the average of the companies in the same sector.

- The extravagant lifestyle of the CEO and the many easy loans to officers.

- Too many and too costly reconstructing charges.

- Earnings have been restated too many times.

- Deceptive accounting practices have been discovered.

- A successful product from the competitor or the current product is losing its market share or becoming a low-profit commodity.

- Insiders and/or institutional investors are dumping the companies' stocks far more than the averages especially in heavy volumes and by more than one insider.

    o Have more than one insider dumping a lot of the stock within a month and no insider purchase in that month.

    o Have more than one insider decrease their holdings by more than 10%.
- The entire stock market is plunging as indicated by our chart in detecting market crash.
- The stock price does not move up with good news. It shows the price has peaked.
- The accumulation amount is far less than the sold amount. When the stock price is up, the accumulation is less than the sold stocks when the stock price was down last time. It indicates no more accumulation ahead and hence the stock will be down most likely.
- Management deteriorates. One hint is the deteriorating ROE from the last quarter.
- Poor operations. They include recalls of products such as the GM recall on ignition switches, product secrets being stolen and customers' credit card info being stolen.

Selling a winner
Even with the above, you may still hesitate to sell a winning horse. It is human nature. Set a stop loss (say 10% below the current price) mentally. You want to do it mentally as you want to avoid flash crashes or events you do not have control of such as 911. You do not want to sell your stocks in such events. Adjust the stop loss price when the stock price rises. You will benefit for rising stocks by not existing prematurely. In another words, let the winners rise.

You define the conditions of a previous peak by using SMA-200% or SMA-50% (from Finviz.com), RSI(14) and P/E. Sell the stock(s) when these conditions happen.

Alternatively, sell the stock when it is in or past the upper Bollinger band if you feel the stock will not have a breakout (i.e. price crosses above the resistance level).

You may have two rights for every wrong prediction of the price direction. Most investors should take profits. It is easier to make 50% on a stock and find another stock to gain 35% than making 100% in the same stock. Of course, there are exceptions.

Remember that the fall of a stock is usually faster and steeper than the rise. Do not fall in love with any stock.

Afterthoughts

- Another article on this topic.
  http://buzz.money.cnn.com/2013/04/05/stocks-sell/
  An article from Investopedia. Nothing new but it is worth to have the same second opinion.
  http://www.investopedia.com/financial-edge/0412/5-tips-on-when-to-sell-your-stock.aspx

It also depends on your strategies. I sell most of my stocks in my momentum portfolio within a month. At least one strategy I know does not keep any stocks during the peak stage of the market cycle – the easiest time to make money but also the riskiest time.

7   Selling a winner

Let the profit rise and at the same time protect your profit. Tesla quadrupled its value in 6 months. Examples abound such as Amazon and Yelp.

You do not want to sell these rocket stocks even if their fundamentals do not make sense. Buffett does not touch these stocks and he usually misses these big gains. However, many of these rocket stocks such as BRRY (Blackberry) will eventually fall losing most of their value. I bet the institutional investors move the market in either direction and usually they read the same analysts' reports. You profit as a contrarian if you have a good reason to act against the herd.

The following example uses a 10% trailing stop. Set the stop at 10% of the current price (i.e. 10% less than the current price), not the purchase price. You need to change the stop when the price rises but do not change it when the price falls. Review your stops every month or more frequently if time allows.

To illustrate, when the stock price rises to 100, set the stop at 90. When the stock price falls to 90, sell the stock at the market price. When the stock price rises to 200, change the stop at 180.

The stop should also be set according to how volatile the stock is. Some stocks are more volatile than others. Most charts show the resistance line. This line assumes the stock price should not fall below this line in normal fluctuations. Set the stop at 2% below this line so your stock will not be stopped out in theory.

To avoid flash crashes, do not place stop orders. Instead, do it mentally (mental stop is my term). When you see that the stock falls below your stop with no sign of a flash crash, sell the stock using a market order.

Of course, there is no bullet-proof scheme. This one should work in the long run. This is my suggestion only, so examine whether it works for you. Small cap and/or stocks with small average volumes fluctuate more.

Examples
I have too many bad examples of selling the stocks too early and sometimes holding them too long.

I made over 40% in a few weeks on ALU, but it went up more than 300% in the next two years. It was acquired in early 2016 by Nokia paying a good premium. I was right that ALU had a lot of valuable patents and I was wrong to dump it when I found out Cisco did not have any intention to acquire it – a big mistake by Cisco and the U.S.

FOSL is another example to teach us to use mental stop loss. FOSL was priced at $33.70 on 1/4/2010. Its fundamentals were just fine with an expected E/P (expected earnings yield) at 6% but decreasing earnings. It gained 115% later in 2010 - not expected.

On 1/3/2011, the expected E/P was still at around 6% and improving earnings. It gained 9% for the year – a little disappointing.

On 1/3/2012, the expected E/P was 7% and a huge earnings growth. Now, we expected a better performance for the year and it did by gaining 20%.

On 1/3/2013, the expected E/P was about 6% and the earnings gain was respectable. It gained 28% to $121. So far, so good.

On 1/2/2014, the E/P and the earnings growth were about the same as in 1/3/2013. However, it lost 7% for the year while SPY (an ETF simulating the market) gained 12%. There was no warning. Did the institutional investors lose the interest of this stock?

On 1/2/2015, the E/P was 7% and the earnings growth was about the same as the previous year. It lost 69% (vs. SPY's 0% return with dividends)!

From 1/4/2010 to 1/3/2016, the annualized return of FOSL is 0% (vs. SPY's 13%). Actually, after dividends, SPY should have an annualized return of about 15%. The lessons gained here are:

- Fundamentals (using EP and earnings growth in this example) may not always work. Otherwise, 2015 should have the same gain as 2014.

- The rosy outlook of the stock may be priced in already. When the outlook fails to materialize, the stock tanks.

8   Tax avoidance

Tax avoidance is a good way to save some money legally. Tax laws change all the time. Check Wikipedia on current investment taxes. Consult your tax lawyer and my knowledge in taxes is limited.

Some even went to the length by using life support to prolong the lives for several weeks so to qualify better estate tax exemption in the following year. Do not implement what I did as tax laws change frequently and every one's situation is different. Here are what I did and hope they will be applicable to you.

- Sold most profitable stocks that I owned more than 12 months in taxable accounts in 2011. I bought some back. I maintained a 15% tax bracket, so the tax bill from Uncle Sam is virtually 0 (not exactly due to more tax on social security and Medicare as a result of the trades). I still had to pay state tax. As a retiree, I can control my income.

    I bet this is the same trick Romney and Buffett used to pay their taxes at low rates.

- Converted part of my Rollover IRA to Roth in 2012 and 2013. I paid taxes today. However, the Roth conversion gives me tax-free appreciation for the trades in this account and it will lower tax and my minimum withdrawal requirement in the future.

- The taxes from dividends in the retirement accounts are deferred but eventually they will be treated as regular income when they are withdrawn. Very few have higher incomes during their retirement. If you are the lucky few due to the successful investing in your retirement accounts, you may end up with higher tax bracket during your retirement, particularly when you are forced to withdraw at age 70 ½.

- Gifted some appreciated stocks to my children. Good for them and not good for Uncle Sam. You can gift up to $14,000 (in 2015) for each spouse to each child without paying any Federal tax. For a family of four, you and your spouse can gift up to $56,000 (= 14,000 * 4) a year in 2015.

    The cost basis of the transferred stock is quite complicated. Check out the current tax law. The cost basis of the appreciated stocks are carried to the receiver, so it would lower your capital taxes as most of us are in higher tax bracket than our children.

From my experience, the cost basis of the depreciated stocks after the transfer is the market price on the transfer day as of 2016. I do not understand it enough to comment but just tell what I have experienced. I tried to offset my son's unexpected short-term capital gain by transferring a losing stock and that does not work.

- My lawyer set up trusts for me including my house. They will avoid probate hopefully. From the current tax law (as of 2016), the cost basis of your stocks will be stepped up or down to the stock prices of that day you pass away. Ask your heirs to keep a business paper for the stock prices or tell your brokers to adjust the cost basis on the day you pass away (send him an e-mail from hell or heaven depending on your new residence LOL). Of course, you have to tell your heirs now to take care of these tasks without using the described email. Again, ask your tax lawyer for details.

  Make sure you specify the beneficiaries in your and your spouse's accounts to avoid probate. Check your local state laws. Some states take more than a year to finish the probate process for a house. As of 2014, my state (Mass.) has an exemption of 1 million, not portable to your spouse, and they calculate the entire estate when it exceeds the exemption. There is no estate tax if my estate is a million dollar. I have to pay a rate on 1,000,001 if it just exceeds it by one dollar. That's why we should move 30 miles north to New Hampshire.

  I estimate that it takes about three years for the average estate to be distributed. You want to cut down the duration by having a will to start, so you do not want to pay extra to your lawyer.

- At age 70 ½ (as of 2016), you are required to withdraw them in a schedule and it could put you in higher tax bracket. Roth withdrawal is not counted in the mandatory withdrawal for a person's lifetime as of 2016.

- Roth IRA if qualified could be the best deal.

- I simulate my next year via my tax preparation software and adjust my income accordingly.

- To avoid the extra tax filing such as some oil partnerships, buy them in your non-taxable accounts.

Afterthoughts

- Tax audit signs.
  http://money.cnn.com/gallery/pf/taxes/2014/03/14/tax-audit/index.html?iid=HP_LN
  To summarize, you're supposed to fill a form (8283) when the donation exceeds $500. Your business would be treated as a hobby if you do not have a profit in three out of the last five years. Check the current tax laws.

- Joke on Romney.
  http://www.tonyp4idea.blogspot.com/2012/11/from-air-force-one-to-prison-one.html

- As of 2013, the dividend tax is 20% max. Do not believe it is no tax in tax-deferred accounts. When you withdraw, it will be treated as a regular income and it can be as high as almost 40% (as of 2013). Your dividend tax rate depends on your income.

- When you trade 5 times or more a week, investigate whether you're eligible to trade as a business by the current tax rule. A business allows its owner to deduct business expenses.

- Fidelity: Investment tax.
  https://www.fidelity.com/learning-center/mutual-funds/tax-implications-bond-funds

  ETF Taxes on Foreign Stocks:
  http://seekingalpha.com/article/2491465-foreign-withholding-taxes-in-international-equity-etfs

- Avoid wash sales in your taxable accounts
  http://en.wikipedia.org/wiki/Wash_sale

9   Trade plan

You should have a trade plan. It should include the following basics:

1. Objective.
2. When, what stocks and how many to buy.
3. When and what stocks to sell.
4. When and how to monitor your trading strategies.

The follow is my suggestion. Adjust them according to your personal requirements.

Be disciplined

It would make your trading to be a discipline which will provide better results in the long run and save you time. Following the trade plan would not allow your emotion to take over.

To illustrate, you have a specific day (Monday or the first day of the month) to check the value of your portfolio. Checking it several times a day is a waste of energy and it could cause harm to your emotions.

Objective

Set up your objective and requirements first. Your objective could be seeking the highest profit, profit at the least risk, protecting principle, generating income or a combination. Beating the market should not be your primary objective.

For example, a better objective is making more than 5% per year in the next 10 years at the least risk. Why 5%? I estimate we have 3% inflation and 2% taxes.

You can be conservative and aggressive at the same time by setting up two accounts, one for each objective. In addition, you may want to define the maximum investment amount for each account.
I have three objectives and they usually fall into different accounts and different holding periods.

- Profit at the least risk. Buy value stocks. Review bought stocks every 6 months. Non-taxable account.

- Momentum. Buy momentum stocks for maximum short-term (1 month) profits. Roth account.
- Conservative. Define a larger safety net. Conserve cash. Move all to stocks only when the market is most favorable.

Contrary to the above, most investors' or traders' objective is beating the market by a specific percent. It is fine too to measure how you perform against the market. For ultra conservative investors, not losing money is the primary objective.

If you made 10% and the market was up by 20%, you did not do good performance wise. However, do not blame yourself if your primary objective is conserving wealth. Most likely you had a high percent of your portfolio in cash and/or safer investments which do not appreciate a lot but they conserve your wealth.

Be flexible

Every one's trade plan is different. You should start a simple one and add features that would be useful to you. Keep it simple as you will not follow a complicated one.

Other features are: how you screen stocks, your average holding period, tax consequences, performance monitor, etc. This chapter shows you the very basics of a trade plan and you should start one if you do not have one.

You can refer to any chapter of this book in your trade plan. To illustrate, refer to the chapters when to sell a stock and spotting market plunges.

You can change your objective. When the market is risky, you want to be more conservative for example.

Disciplined but adaptive

Stick with the plan consistently. When your strategy that has been proven before does not work now, you should still stick to it. It is a common mistake for traders switching different technical indicator when the current one does not work. It explains why most beginner traders lose money.

It should be adaptive. When the current market favors growth, stick with a growth strategy.

A sample trade plan

You can review what stocks to buy and sell once a week or once a month depending on how active you are in the market. List the criteria you want to buy. Define your average holding period for a specific objective. Also define when and why you want to sell a stock.

Personally I prefer to have two sections: Common Tasks and Specific Tasks. Common Tasks includes 4 categories: Weekly Tasks, Monthly Tasks, Quarterly Tasks and Yearly Tasks. Evaluate stocks to buy on Tuesday every week for example. Update the portfolio and check out the chart on marketing timing on the first week of every month. Review performance of the portfolio quarterly (or half a year). Perform year-end tasks.

Specific Tasks include tasks I have to do on specific dates such as filing tax return, transferring stocks to my children and renewing investing subscriptions.

Weekly Tasks:

Mon	Covered calls
	IBD-50 review
Tue	Momentum strategy
Wed	Sell Momentum stocks over 2 weeks.

Monthly Tasks:

Mon	Performance monitor.
	Market timing: Market & Correction.
Tue	Find stocks using selected strategies.
	Find stocks using screens.
Wed	Evaluate stocks
Thur.	Buy stocks
	Sector rotation.
Fri	Evaluate any stocks to sell.
Any	Monitor momentum performance.

Quarterly Tasks:

1	Monthly tasks.
2	Performance monitor.

Year-end Tasks:

1	Tax adjustments for taxable accounts.
2	EOY purchases.
3	Spreadsheet for taxable accounts.
4	Fully invested in Dec. 15-Jan. 15
5	Screen performance monitor.
6	Dogs of DOW.

Review your performance and the trade plan

If you do not know what you did, how can you know what you're going? Review every trade transaction and monitor their performances.

Learn from your losses. Did you stick to the trade plan? If you lose too many times and/or take too much risk (evidenced by many losses and/or big losses), you may have to modify your trade plan. However, the trade plan may not be good to the current market (for example trading growth stocks in the bottom of the market cycle).

If you have to let the winners get away too often, review what's wrong. Sometimes, a lesson is not a lesson but just bad luck.

Learn about yourself

Learn about your risk tolerance, how mentally prepared are you on big losses and big wins. If you have more money than you can use for the rest of your life, conserving wealth should be your primary objective.

To illustrate with a portfolio of one million, your average stock position is $100,000 if you only have time to follow 10 stocks.
To many, the portfolio with 10 stocks is quite risky. You may consider having 10 stocks of $50,000 each and invest the rest ($500,000) in ETFs, mutual funds and/or bonds. Ensure no three or more stocks (some prefer 2) are in the same sector.

Prepare for some losses. Reduce the average loss to small amounts. I prefer 25% maximum loss for volatile stocks and 20% for other stocks. Some prefer using stop loss orders of 10% to 15% loss. Today's market is too volatile to stop losses less than 15%. One's opinion. You should have some big winners but let them getting away by selling them too early. One way is to use stop orders (10% less than the market price) and adjust the stops periodically (say a month) for the appreciating stocks.

A quick way

Write down your objective and what tasks you do every week, month and year in the inside back cover in this book (hard copy only). If you do not do it now, you will never do it.

Trade journal

Keep a journal of your trades and ideas. Review it from time to time why you bought a specific stock. It is far better than recalling the experiences from memory.

Everyone should have a book such as this one to record their experiences. I do not recommend publishing one. You should spend your time in investing. Unless you're famous, most likely publishing is not profitable.

It should be part of a trade plan. You use it to monitor your performance of your trade. When you use a screen that is for short term, you want to exit the trade accordingly. When the screen does not perform, it may mean the market is not favorable to this screen and you should skip using it with actual money. Here is a screenshot of mine. I group the trades under different screens.

	A	B	C	D	E	F	G	H	I	J	K	L	M	N	O	P
1	Performance			Price		$					Date			Return		Status
2	Stock	QTY	Account	B.P.	S.P.	Buy $	Sell $	Profit	Curr P.	% better	Buy Date	Sell Date	Days		Ann. Ret	
3	LAKE	2,000	401K	10.93	13.99	21,860	27,975	6,115	9.45	48%	07/15/15	11/24/15	132	28%	77%	S
4	ABTL	1,500	ROTH	16.60	18.50	24,900	27,750	2,850			07/16/15	09/10/16	422	11%	10%	B
5	ELMD	5,000	401K	4.01	4.22	20,054	21,095	1,041	4.81	-12%	03/17/16	04/07/16	21	5%	90%	S

The formulae are:
B.P. (Buy Price) =IF(B3="","",IF(D3="","",D3*B3))
% better =IF(I3="","",(E3-I3)/I3)
Days =IF(K3="","",L3-K3)
Return =IF(D3="","",(E3-D3)/D3)
Ann. Ret =IF(N3="","",N3*365/M3)

Add any columns you want such as Account.

Section V: Market timing

Chapter 2 is the only required reading for now in this section.

Investing from 1970 to 2000 enjoys an average annual return of about 10% and market timing is a waste of time and actually reduces the performance by parking too much cash. Since 2000, the market has changed. As of 5/2014, we have two major market plunges with an average loss of over 45%. The apples you picked are sour but some other times are tasty from the same tree. You just pick them in the wrong time or in the right time.

Market timing is about educated guesses unless you have a time machine ☺. Hopefully we will have more rights than wrongs when we follow general guidelines. It would reduce risk and could benefit us financially in the long run.

The following chapter helps you to time the market in the simplest term. It is followed by several related chapters. Just the first one and try it out. Skip the rest in section for now, which is used as a reference or read it later.

Tip

	SMA-50	SMA-200	SMA-350	SMA50/SMA200	RSI (14)
Market					
Peak		5%	9%	101%	65%
Bottom		-32%	-31%	78%	25%
Correction					
Peak	4%	6%	11%	102%	65%
Bottom	-5%	-6%	-7%	97%	26%
Stock					
Peak					70%
Bottom					30%

SMA350% = (Stock Price − SMA) / SMA
where SMA is Single Moving Average for 350 sessions

1 The power of market timing

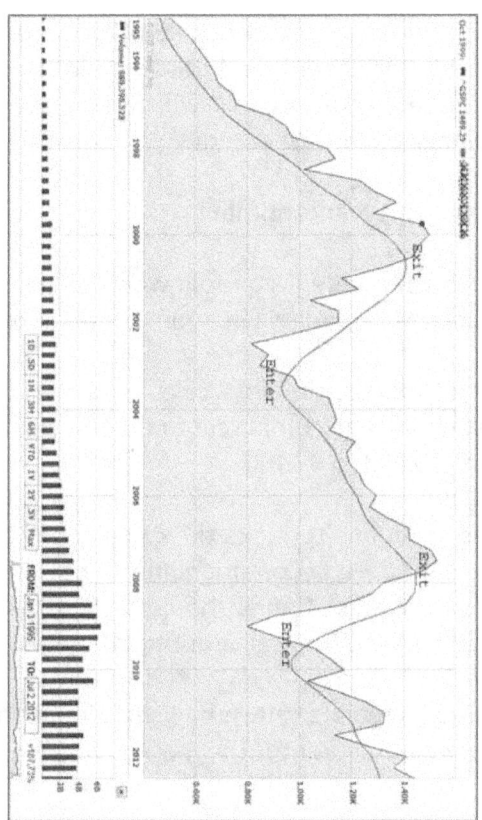

Most e-book readers allow you to select the graph to make it fit entirely to your screen. Detecting market plunges indicates the exit points and reentry points from 2000 to 9-2009 as follows.

Table: Vital Dates

Market Plunge	Peak	Bottom	Indicator Exit	Indicator Reenter
2000	08/28/00	09/20/02	10/01/00	06/01/03
2007	10/12/07	03/06/09	02/01/08	09/01/09
			08/01/11	11/01/11

As of 04/2014, my chart (from Yahoo!Finance) still indicates to invest fully in the market. For simplicity I skip a few brief exits and reentries since 2011. Run the simple chart once a month. When it indicates a potential market plunge is closer, run the chart once a week.

It is based on stock prices so it may not identify the peaks and bottoms precisely, but so far it has never failed to avoid big losses and ensure big gains by reentering the market. Hope it will give us enough time to act in the next market plunge as the last two did.

Unbelievable return with market timing

Calculate how much you made if you followed the above exit points and reenter points from 2000 to today. I bet you would make a good fortune.

To test the effect of market timing, I calculated the return of S&P 500 stocks with market timing and compare it to the return of S&P 500 without market timing from 1-2000 to 9-2013.

There are many assumptions to make the calculations easier. In general, dividends are not considered. Compounding is not considered in most cases. The return with market timing should be substantially better if we buy a contra ETF during exits and sell it during reentries.

I was shocked by the incredible return by using simple market timing and the chart tells us to exit and reenter the market only 3 times from 2000 to 2013.

Summary info:

S&P 500 1-2000 to 9-2013	With Market Timing	Without Market Timing
Better	500%	
Gain	1,000	167
Gain %	68%	11%
Annualized gained	5%	1%
Days	4,959	4,959

Calculations:

S & P 500	With Market Timing	Without Market Timing
1-2000	1,469[1]	1,469[1]
Exit 10/01/00	1,041[2]	1,041
Enter 06/01/03	1,041	964[4]
Exit 02/01/08	1,489[3]	1,379[4]
Enter 09/01/09	1489	1,020[5]

Exit 08/01/11	1,888	1,293
Enter 11/01/11	1,888	1,251
09/03/13	2,469	1.638
Gained	2,469 – 1,469=1,000	1,638-1,469=167
Gain %	1000/1469 = 68%	167/1469 = 11%
Annualized gained	68% * 365/4959=5%	11%*365/4959=1%
Better	(1,000-167)/167 = 500%	

Portfolio with Market Timing:

[1] Both start with S&P 500 of 1,469 on 1-3-2000.
[2] 10/01/00
The market timing portfolio exits the market and remains same value of 1,041 until 6/1/00.
[3] 02/01/08
The market timing portfolio exits the market and remains same value of 1,489 until 9/1/09.

'1,489' is calculated as follows:
1,041 * (1 + Rate) = 1,041 * (1 + 1,379-964)/964) = 1,489
where S&P 500 is 964 on 6/1/00 and 1,379 on 2/1/08.

The other calculations are based on S&P 500 is 1,020 on 9/1/9, 1,293 on 8/1/11, 1,251 on 11/1/11 and 1,636 on 9/3/13.

Portfolio without Market Timing:

[1] Both starts with S&P 500 of 1,469 on 1-3-2000. We could use the S&P 500 value on 9/3/13, but it will not account on some compounded interest consideration.

[4] S&P 500 is 964 in 6/1/00 and 1,379 on 2/1/08.

[5] 02/01/08. The portfolio value is calculated to be 1,020 as follows:
1,379 * (1 + Rate) = 1,379 * (1 + (1020-1379)/1379) = 1,020
where S&P 500 is 1,379 on 2/1/08 and 1,020 on 9/1/09.

The other calculations are based on S&P 500 is 1,293 on 8/1/11, 1,251 on 11/1/11 and 1,636 on 9/3/13.

I cannot believe the shocking return with market timing. I checked my calculation and there was nothing wrong but do not hold me on this. Ignoring the compound rate of return should be minor. If you have time, send me your e-mail address to pow_tony@yahoo.com, so I can send you the spreadsheet to check out any error.

Even if I made a mistake somehow and got 100% instead of 500%, it still doubles the return without market timing! Ask any fund manager what it means to his or her fund performance and his / her career.

It will detect the next market plunges, but it may not give us ample of time to react as the last two did. It will not detect the precise bottoms and peaks as they depend on the stock price of an ETF representing the market. I have separate statistics on market peaks and bottoms but they have not been proven. The above may not work as effectively if there are too many followers. On the contrary it may work as it could be a self-fulfilling prophesy.

The stock prices of SPY are obtained from Yahoo!Finance. The entry and exit points are obtained from my simple chart from Yahoo!Finance described and they are subject to my interpretation.

#Filler: Miss Mia

In my first job just after the Vietnam War, every one tried to date my beautiful office mate Mia except me. If we married, then her name would be Mia Pow. She would be very popular, or very unpopular without showing her beautiful face. In any case, when she becomes a mother, she will be Mamma Mia.

BTW. I was the "comfort man" due to the gender gap during the Vietnam War.

2   Market cycle

"Bull markets are born on pessimism, grow on skepticism, mature on optimism, and die on euphoria" - Sir John Templeton

The stock market has cycles as our practical interpretation of the above. It is about five years apart, but it fluctuates widely. I divide it into four stages: Bottom, Early Recovery, Up and Peak.

My defined four stages of a market cycle

We need to apply the right investing strategies to each of the four stages of the cycle.

- **Bottom**

    I would not invest for at least the first six months (or even a year) after the big plunge starts, which could lose over 25% in a few months. The exceptions are investing in contra ETFs and selling short for aggressive investors.

    I estimate it will take a year from the start of the plunge to the bottom, so I will normally sell stocks early in the plunge and do not buy stocks that are in the sector (sometimes sectors) that causes the bubble for about two years after the plunge.

    At the bottom, the high-yield corporate bonds (i.e. junk bonds) would prosper when the interest rates is decreasing to stimulate the economy.

    From mid-2007 to mid-2008, bonds suffered as the investors thought the sky was falling down - it was to those who lost the jobs and/or their houses. After that, some bonds especially the long-term bonds appreciated about 50% for the following year.

    The government lowered the interest rates and these bond prices with high interest rates surged. Correct timing in buying bonds could be very profitable.

    Long-term bonds have more impact by the interest rate: The lower the interest rate, the higher the bond prices of higher-yield bonds. The older bonds with higher interest rates are more valuable to the newer bonds with lower interest rates.

I define this period of the bottom from the start of the plunge to the start of Early Recovery.

- **Early Recovery**

    It usually starts after one year from the plunge; no one can pinpoint the exact time consistently. By this time preferably earlier, we should have closed out all positions in contra ETFs and shorts.

    Roughly speaking, October, 2007 (some use 2008) is the start of the market plunge. March, 2009 is the end of the bottom stage and the start of the early recovery stage of the 2007 cycle. However, every market cycle is different in where it starts and ends.

    The one-year gain from the bottom is most profitable. It usually gains over 25% in a year from the market bottom. I, a conservative investor, had huge gains using some leverage in my largest taxable account in 2009. From my memory, I had a similar return in 2003 but I had not saved the statement as in 2009.

    In this phase, value is a better parameter than growth in searching for stocks. If your investment subscription provides a composite value score and a composite timing score, the sort parameter of your screened stocks could be "Composite Value / Composite Timing" in descending order. Select the top stocks in this order. You still have to analyze the top-screened stocks.

    Forward (same as Expected) P/E is a good metric. However, most companies may be losing money at this stage. Those companies that can last for more than one year with its cash reserve are potential good buys. The best appreciated stocks are beaten companies that have precious technologies and good customer bases. They could be candidates to be acquired if they are small enough.

- **Up**

    Usually the growth metrics such as PEG could be better than the value metrics such as expected P/E during this phase. Most stocks are winners except contra ETFs and shorting stocks. When the growth stocks are making headlines and the defensive stocks are being dumped, this is the hint that we're well into the Up phase of the market cycle.

Locate stocks with growth metrics such as favorable PEG and high SMA-200% (from Finviz.com). Do not be scared on how much they have already appreciated. The strategy "Buy High and Sell Higher" works in this phase. Protect your profits with stops.

Ensure that they have value too. Skip the stocks with expected P/Es higher than 35 unless there are good reasons. Most stocks will gain due to the tide of the market. However, when they're overbought (RSI(14) over 60), be careful. When institutional investors sell these stocks, they will crash.

- **Peak**

  When everyone makes easy money and the interest rates is high, watch out. Stop loss and/or stop limit should be used to protect your investment. Check out whether there is any bubble that would be burst like the internet in 2000 and the finance (and housing) in 2007.

  Internet crisis is easy to spot, but not the financial crisis. In 2007 we had a cycle longer than the average which is about 5 years. The plunge is very fast and very steep – thanks to the institutional investors who drive the market down.

  Run the technical analysis chart described in the Chapter on Spotting Big Market Plunges at least monthly (weekly if you have time). Protect your investment. Do not fall in love with any stock (you can buy it back later at a deep discount). Making the last buck is a fool's game.

  Accumulate cash according to your risk tolerance. A retiree or a conservative investor would accumulate from 25% to 50% and should be ready to move to all cash when the plunge starts.

  We can lower the cash percent if we use enough stop loss protection. Be psychologically prepared because the stock market may still rise for a while. There is no perfect market timing.

The 2007 Cycle

The market plunged starting in 10-2007 and ending in 3-2009 (bottom), started to recover in 3-2009 (early recover), and trended up from 2010 to 1-2013 (the up phase of the market cycle). As of 3/2016, it is the peak phase defined by me.

As of 1/2013, we have recovered all the market losses since 2007. However, as of 7/2014, the economy has not fully recovered compared to the economy before the plunge. The employment judging by the medium salary has not fully recovered and the economy is not expanding. It is uncommon that the economy does not follow the market. It is due to the excessive supply of money by the government and partly due to globalization to allow companies to hire overseas.

Although a W-shaped recession seldom happens, we have a chance today. We hope we do not have a depression and/or the similar lost decades that Japan has been experiencing. Some may conclude we are close to completing a market cycle from 2007 to 2016. As of 2016, the economy is recovering slowly and we're better than most other global economies.

Again, market timing is not an exact science as it involves irrational human beings and government interventions. The timing using market cycle described here is a guideline as it is hard to time it exactly.

The average market cycle is about 5 years, but they fluctuate. If we consider 2007 as the plunge, we have about 8 years of this cycle as of 2015.

In a typical cycle (few are typical), we have about one year in each of the 4 phases I defined (plunge, early recovery, up and peak).

Events/Triggers

There are financial events and triggers that cause the transition of one phase of the market cycle to another. They usually do not change the sequence of the phases (say not from Peak to Early Recovery), but they may change the duration of the phase. Examples are:
- The government announcing change of the interest rate,
- Change of employment, and
- Change of GNP.

Sectors in a market cycle (my suggestion)

Market Phase	Favorable	Unfavorable
Early Recovery	Financial, Technology, Industrial	Energy, Telecom, Utilities
Up	Technology, Industrial, Housing	
Peak	Mineral, Health Care, Energy, Long-Term Bond, Consumer Discretionary	
Bottom	Consumer Staples, Utilities	Consumer Discretionary, Technology, Industrial, Long-Term & high-yield Bond

The sectors that cause the recession usually take a longer time to recover. In 2000, the technology sector was not favorable in the Early Recovery phase, contrary to the above table. In 2007, the financial sector was not favorable in the Early Recovery phase. These are the "offending" sectors that cause the plunges.

In a recession, we usually cannot cut down on consumer staples and utilities, but we can cut down on buying consumer gadgets. Companies usually postpone investing in equipment and systems during a recession and expand when the economy is humming. The government usually lowers the interest rates right after the plunge to stimulate the economy.

Conclusion

When the market is about to plunge or change from one stage to another, run the described chart more frequently and read more articles written by the experts. Again, market timing is not an exact science but it is based on educated guesses. The better guesses should have more rights than wrongs in the long term. Our actions depend on our risk tolerance. Be careful on using any new strategy that has not been fully understood and proven. Since 2000, market timing is very important to your financial health with two market plunges with an average of about 45% loss.

3 Calendar Timing

I made the following charts so it is easier to time the market by calendar.

All dates are inclusive.

No.	Metric		Score
1	Seasonal	Nov. - April, Score = 1	
2	Best Month	Nov., Score = 1	
		Sep., Score = -1	
3	Best Days	Dec. 15 – Jan.15 Score = 1	
4	Presidential Cycle	Election Year, Score = 1	
		1st Year in Office, Score = -1	
		2nd year, Score = -1	
		3rd year, Score = 2	
5	Market Cycle[1]	Plunging, Score = -3	
		Early Recovery, Score = 3	
		Up, Score = 2	
		Peak, Score = 1	
		Grand Score	

Footnote.
1   Refer to the Market Cycle chapter on how I define phases of a cycle.

Add up all the scores. The passing grade for the grand score is 1 but I have not really tested out past performance. It is the first time you see a scoring system on market timing combining.

Sectors for market cycle

Market Phase[1]	Favorable	Unfavorable
Early Recovery	Financial, Technology, Industrial	Energy, Telecom, Utilities
Up	Technology, Industrial	
Peak	Mineral, Health Care, Energy	
Bottom	Consumer Staples, Utilities	Consumer Discretionary, Technology, Industrial

Seasonal	Favorable	Unfavorable
Winter	Energy, Utilities	
End of year	QQQ, EWG	
Olympics	ETF for host country[2]	

Footnote.
2   Refer to Market Cycle chapter on how I define phases of a cycle.
Buy it next year after Olympics. It could be due to higher GDP or the publicity. However, be selective. Greece is too small a country to host an Olympics.

3   Buy it next year after Olympics. It could be due to higher GDP or the publicity. However, be selective. Greece is too small a country to host an Olympics.

Summary

I made the following charts so it is easier to time the market by calendar.

All dates are inclusive.

No.	Metric		Score
1	Seasonal	Nov. - April, Score = 1	
2	Best Month	Nov., Score = 1	
		Sep., Score = -1	
3	Best Days	Dec. 15 – Jan.15 Score = 1	
4	Presidential Cycle	Election Year, Score = 1	
		1st Year in Office, Score = -1	
		2nd year, Score = -1	
		3rd year, Score = 2	
5	Presidential[3]	Democratic = 1 Republican = -1	
6	Market Cycle	Early Recovery, Score = 3	
		Up, Score = 2	
		Peak, Score = 1	
7	SPY (Finviz.com)	SMA200% > 8%[2] Score = -1	
		SMA200% < 0 Score = -1	
		RSI(14) > 65% Score = -1	
		Grand Score	

Footnote.
2 Refer to Market Cycle chapter on how I define phases of a cycle.
3 For simplicity, use Finviz.com. Enter SPY and you will find SMA200% and RSI(14) to predict whether the market is peaking and overbought.
4 I'm political neutral. The selection is based on historical statistics.

Add up all the scores. The passing grade is 0. According to my table which is based on my personal selections/preferences, the market is favorable when the grand score is 1 or higher. I bet it is the first time you see such a scoring system for market timing.

Sectors for market cycle

Market Phase	Favorable		Unfavorable
Early Recovery	Financial, Technology, Industrial		Energy, Telecom, Utilities
Up	Technology, Industrial		
Peak	Mineral, Health Care, Energy		
Bottom	Consumer Staples, Utilities		Consumer Discretionary, Technology, Industrial
Seasonal	**Favorable**		**Unfavorable**
Winter	Energy, Utilities		
End of year	QQQ, EWG		
Olympics	ETF for host country[2]		

4   Politics and investing

You may ask why politics is discussed in this investing book. Politics has been proven to affect the market. For example, the market had reacted to the different stages of Quantitative Easing whose dates had been preset. The following is a more recent example.

I predicted 2015 would be a year with small profit and insisted on so even during the fierce correction in August. Why I was so sure? Very seldom the market is down in a year before an election year including 2007. The last occurrence was 1939, the year when WW2 started. Investing is a multi-discipline venture including statistics and politics. It may not always happen, but the probability is high for these years.

How to profit

2015 was a sideward market. The market reacted to good news and bad news. The strategy for sideway market is: Buy at temporary downs and sell at temporary peaks. Define 'temporary' according to your risk tolerance.

For the 'temporary market down', personally I used 5% down from the last market peak. To me the 'temporary market peak' is 10% up from the last market down. The percentages can apply to the percentage changes in the stocks in your watch list. In another words, I buy the stock when the market is 5% down from the last peak and sell it when it gains 10% or the market gains 10%. Be reminded that this strategy is opposite to market plunges, where you should exit the market totally - again depending on your risk tolerance.

The following are my purchases on 08/26/2015. I should have bought more stocks and one day earlier if I were not blinded by fears (a human nature) during this correction. Here is my proof for my purchase orders. The four stocks were described as value stocks in a SA article and I did a simple evaluation. As of 12/31/2015, I sold all the four stocks except Gilead Sciences. The annualized returns are more impressive such as GNW's 10% gain in one day.

Stocks	Buy Price	Buy Date	Return	Sold date
Apple (AAPL)	107.20	08/26/15	12%	10/19/15
Gilead Sciences (GILD)	105.94	08/26/15	-4%	
General Motors (GM)	27.69	08/26/15	12%	09/17/15
Genwealth Financial (GNW)	4.54	08/26/15	10%	08/27/15

There were similar examples in 2013 and 2014.

2016: Politics and the market

No one including all the Federal Reserve chairmen / chairwomen and all the Nobel-Prize winners in economics can predict market plunges. One chairman predicted a smooth market and a few months later the housing market crashed. Many predicted correctly market crashes by pure luck. One even received a Nobel Prize and became famous. However, you are glad to ignore his later market predictions.

There are at least two best sellers asking us to exit the market in 2009. If you followed them, you would miss all the big gains from 2009 to 2014. They did have a point. However, you cannot fight the Fed. The market had been saved by the excessive printing of money and hence created a non-correlation between the market and the economy. I bet these authors (famous economists and gurus) may have not made a buck in the stock market. It is a classic case of the blind leading the blind.

From their articles, they do not know the basic technical indicator. You only want react to the market when the market is plunging and not too early. That's why most fund managers cannot beat the market as most are not allowed to time the market. Buffett had mediocre returns in the last three years – I had warned my readers three years ago in my blogs/books. To me, the 'buy-and-hold' strategy is dead since 2000. The average loss from the peak for the last two market plunges is about 45%. Most charts depend on falling prices, so you will not save 45% and 25% loss is my objective.

Fundamentally speaking

The market in 2016 is risky due to the proposed interest rates hike, our record-high margin, strong U.S. dollar and the high expenses of the wars to start. Each reason could be a good-size article. Personally I try to maintain 50% in cash and would flee the market if my technical indicator tells me so.

Politically (and statistically) speaking

The election year is the second best for the market, but it may not be this year. We seldom have three terms from the same political party. For that, I predict a win by the Republicans. Republicans are usually pro-business, but ironically the democratic presidency has better track record for better market performance.

The market has more than recovered since the day when Obama took office. The S&P 500 performance under Republicans vs. Democrats since 1926 to 2014 is approximately:

   Annualized return under Democratic presidencies: 13%
   Annualized return under Republican presidencies: 6%

The market is riskier based on the above statistics. In addition, there is a good chance that we will have either a non-politician president or a lady president for the first time. The market usually does not favor to this kind of change.

Critical political issue for 2016

On our way back at about 4 pm on a Saturday, the bus was full of Spanish-speaking workers. I bet most are illegal workers working in my suburb such as our malls, the hospital and many restaurants. Why illegals? I bet most legal folks would get welfare instead of working in that shift. If they work, the state would take away the freebies such as health care in Mass. The illegals do not have this option. I do not think the politicians understand this. There is no need for building a border wall but punishing the employers who hire illegals. Before we do this, we need folks to take the jobs taken by the illegals today.

What will happen if the politicians turn the illegals to be legal? There will be nobody doing these jobs I predict. No one in the right mind wants these jobs as it is far easier to collect welfare. Why would politicians make this stupid decision? They want to buy Hispanic votes as evidenced in the last two elections.

In addition, most politicians side with the welfare recipients. Since 40% of the population do not pay Federal taxes, the politicians have to satisfy their needs in order to buy votes.

We should encourage folks to work, not the other way round. Representation without taxation is worse than taxation without representation.

Our high taxes, regulations and strong US dollar dampen our competitive edge.

Some political decisions/regulations that affect the stocks

Beside the presidency and the interest rates hike(s), there are many political decisions and regulations that affect the stocks. Just name a few here:

- The never-ending wars postpone our secular bull market beyond 2018.
- Solar City (SCTY). It depends on government energy credit.
- My Chinese solar panel stock evaporated when the US banned them from importing to the US.
- Any gun control measurement will affect gun stocks.
- Restrictions on cigarettes.
- France imposes extra taxes to foreign investors.
- Government bailouts on 'too big to fall' companies.
- Corporate taxes boost the exodus of corporation headquarters to tax heavens for the US. It is the same for Chinese corporations.
- Infrastructure projects.
- Taking out the ban to export oil would increase the profits for oil companies.
- After the annexation of Crimea, the Congress restricted using Russia's rocket engines and gave new opportunity to the US companies in this

area. Besides political consideration, Chinese rockets are the most cost effective and more reliable.
- China's suppressing corruption affected Macau's casinos...

Summary

Politics affect the market. I predict a risky market in 2016.
Economy and religion also affect the market. Statistically speaking, the market is ahead of the economy by about 6 months. However, the current market is an exception. The correlation will return to normal.

Religions cause wars as the ones in the Middle East today. These huge expenses are consumption, not investing. It will not be good for most sectors of the economy especially in the long run.

Written in 1/1/2016.

Note.

Predictions are predictions. However, the more the educated the guess is, the better chance the guess will materialize. My technical indicator gave only one false alarm from 2000 to 2009. It happens more often after that period. The market is far more volatile than before. In most cases, false alarms will not hurt at all except tax consequences on taxable accounts. The false alarm tells us to exit the market and come back shortly.

5 Market timing example

The market is making new highs. There are always two camps of market timers. One camp predicts a crash is coming while the other predicts it will continue making new highs. This article includes both arguments and suggests how and what actions you need to take to protect your investments.

Management summary

As of 09/22/2018, the market is fundamentally unsound evidenced by fundamental metrics but technically sound evidenced by technical metrics that both will be described in this article.

Suggested actions

No one predicts the market correctly and consistently. Otherwise there are no poor folks. Moving the risky investments such as most stocks to cash too early would miss the potential profits. Moving it too late would risk the loss of your stocks.

Your actions depend on your risk tolerance. If you are conservative such as a retiree, you may want to have a larger portion of your investments in lower risk such as CDs and bonds. You can take one of the following three actions or combine all of the three actions.

1. When the market turns to technically unsound, it is time to move your stocks to cash. The market timing indicators may give false signals. In this case, the indicator would tell you to move back to stocks. Most likely you do not lose much except dealing with the consequences of taxes in non-retirement accounts.
2. Move a portion of your risky investments into cash, laddered CDs and/or short-term bonds. Again, the size of the portion depends on your risk tolerance.
3. Use stops. The sell orders would be changed to market orders when the stocks dip below prices specified by you. I prefer to use SPY or other ETF to determine the market direction. Some sectors and some stocks move faster than others. In one crash, my energy stocks were still profitable while the market was tanking. Eventually these energy stocks caught up and fell fast. Today's highly profitable stocks are FAANG stocks as a group.

I propose and prefer 'manual stop orders' to prevent market manipulation. However, usually large ETFs cannot be manipulated easily. Manipulators try to profit from your stop orders. Set a stop order price in your `mind. When the stock falls to that specified price, sell it via a market order.

My friend confirmed my "manual stop order":

"High-frequency trading via Algo Trading Strategy can see exactly where pre-set trailing stops are and sweep across them (play them) like strings on a violin. Pre-set a trailing stop and it is bound to be triggered because Algo hunt them down. Then watch the market rip higher."

Analysis: Fundamentals and Technical

It consists of Fundamental Analysis and Technical Analysis. The former measures how expensive the current market is and the latter measures the trend of the market.

Many metrics are obtained from Finviz.com as of 9/22/2018 while others are obtained from other websites. With the exception of Fidelity.com, all websites described here are free and readily available. It also serves as a guide on how you can do your own market timing especially after a few months.

The following chart uses SPY to represent the market of the top 500 stocks. It is market cap weighted. It means the higher the market cap the stock, the higher percent of the stock is represented in the index. It turns out most are riskier FAANG stocks.

Enter Finviz.com in your browser and enter SPY. I am not responsible for any errors.

Indicator	Pass	Current Value	Indicating
• Technical			
Death Cross[1]		SMA-50 = 2.3% & SMA-200 = 6.3%	Pass
Technical Analysis: 350 SMA%[2]	>0	Price above the SMA-350.	Pass
RSI(14)	<70	61	Pass
Duration (yr.)	<5	10	Fail
		Overall	**Pass**
• Fundamental			

Valuation			
P/E[3]	<15.7	25.4	High by 62%. Fail.
Shiller P/E[3]	<16.6	33.5	High by 102%. Fail
P/B[3]	<2.78	3.52	High by 27%. Fail.
P/S[3]	<1.50	2.33	High by 55%. Fail.
Oil price	30-100	70.71	Pass
Interest rate[6] T-Bill 1 months[7]	<5	2.05	Pass
T-Bill 3 months[7]	Yield	2.18	
T-Bill 30 years[7]	curve	3.20	Pass
Flow to Equity[4]		-3.371M	Fail
Flow to bond[4]		7.206M	
Corporate debt/GDP[8]	<40	45%	High by 13%. Fail.
USD[5]		Strong	Fail
Gold		High	Fail
Bubble		Several	Fail
Market experts		Fear long term	Neutral
Politics		Trump	Fail
Misc.		Trade war	Fail
		Overall	**Fail**

[1] This is the market timing technique without using a chart.
[2] I tried to use SMA-400% to reduce false signals without success.
[3] Get it from http://www.multpl.com/ (same as CAPE).
[4] Get it from https://www.ici.org/research/stats. It is based on 09-12-18. "Flow to Equity" is based on domestic ETF estimate. Treat it as two phases in moving to equity. First phase of moving excessively to equity indicates the market is peaking. The second phase indicates the market is plunging when flow of equity is excessively negative.
[5] Global corporations will suffer in profits converted back to USD and hard to sell to foreign countries. [4] Get it from the above link.
[6] Rising interest is bad for corporations and high-ticket products, but good for lenders.

[7] Get it from
https://www.treasury.gov/resource-center/data-chart-center/interest-rates/Pages/TextView.aspx?data=yield based on 09/21/18
[8] With the low interest rate, it may not be that critical. Corporations take advantage of the low interest rate.

Overall

Overall, technical is fine as the market is making new highs. Many aggressive investors exit the market on technical indicators only as the over-valued market could linger on for a long term such as from 2009 to 2017 so far.

Overall, fundamental is not sound. The increasing market price also is decreasing the fundamental metrics such as P/E, P/B and P/S. It is bad unless there is reason to support such as the fast earnings growth in 2009.

Many metrics are deteriorating

RSI(14) is getting closer to 70 (a passing grade specified by me).

Inverse yield curve (1.5 vs. 2.33) is about 61% apart from my interpretation and calculation. It is not a warning now but we should keep an eye on it. Most market crashes have occurred when it is 0% or negative. The theory is that in a normal case the short-term interest rates should be lower than the long-term interest rate.

Another source calculates it is 1.1% and that is very close to inversion since the last recession. From MarketWatch, the 30-year fixed interest rates is 4.66% and 1-year rate is 3.96% giving an inverse yield curve 18% apart, which is quite alarming.

Mathematically incorrect, today's full employment is at 4%. Most recessions are closely preceded by troughs in unemployment and the reverse for economy recovery.

GDP growth has been predicted from 1.8% to 3%. The 3% is from the White House for their obvious purpose. I predict it will pop up due to meeting the tariff deadlines, tax cuts and spending increases. It will then be declining to 2%. A healthy US economy should maintain 3% without special factors such as excessive immigration.

We have record debts: investors' margin, corporate debt and Federal debt. These are bubbles going to burst. Federal debt / GDP is about 95% (https://fred.stlouisfed.org/series/gfdegdq188S) today. It does not predict the market performance as this ratio was 53% and 55% before the last two market crashes. It will affect the long-term performance of the economy when we have to service the huge national debt.

We do have 10 years of stock growth at the expense of record Federal deficit. Thanks to President Obama from investors and no thanks from next generations who have to pay back our national debt. It is overdue for a correction. Hopefully it is not a crash which has an average loss of about 45%. We did have two recent corrections losing more than 10%: 2011-12 EU debt crisis and 2014-16 oil crash.

The oil price has been rising from $30 per barrel to today's $70. It is still a long way from my warning of $120.

Potential triggers

Trade wars with China, Canada or EU will be the strongest trigger. Our most profitable companies are virtually all international companies. They need fair trade to prosper.

The other trigger is the possible impeachment of President Trump.

Check the validity of our charts

It seems some metrics vary. It could use after hour trading. It could be the "Days" may be "Sessions" – calendar day is different from trading session. I selected 10 years for most of the charts and StockCharts let me select only 5 years.

Review

This chapter reviews and summarizes important concepts in this book. I am a reader too to remind me on the lessons. This book allows me to write down my ideas and experiences. I review them and monitor how many mistakes I still repeat in investing.

1. A mistake may not be a mistake, or a win may not be a win.

Mistakes are repeated over and over again due to not staying consistently with a solid strategy and letting our emotions to influence our trading.

However, some 'mistakes' are not mistakes. I have evaluated my past trading record to determine whether my money losing episodes are real mistakes, just bad luck on uncontrollable circumstances or bad financial data.

If it is a real mistake, write it down to avoid repeating the same mistake. Often a trading mistake is worth more in future successes than experiencing a one-time windfall. To illustrate, I bought a small Chinese company that had excellent financial metrics, but it was all fraud and I lost most of my money in the stock. After a while, I made the same mistake again.

Cheat me once, shame on you. Cheat me twice, shame on me. I had that shame.

It is the same for a win, but in reverse sense.

For those readers not having the large number (about 100 to 150) of stocks as I do, draw your lessons by including stocks that have been evaluated even they have not been bought.

Overnight my MOS turned from profit into loss due to the collapse of the cartel in potash industry. It is an event we cannot control, expect or will be repeated, so this loss is not a lesson to be learned.

I am guilty of repeating same mistakes such as buying foreign stocks that have been proven not profitable recently.

2. Spotting big plunges.

Market timing does not always work. However, when it works more times than it does not, we can benefit a lot in the long run. Play defensive when the market is risky. Monitor how risky is the market routinely and act accordingly. Set up a schedule when to review market risk. In addition, understand market cycles.

Unless the same strategy is overused, the chart should work. It may not give us ample time to react as the last two. Again, it depends on the data (the stock price), so it will not detect the bottom and the peak precisely, but it will spare you further losses and return in time when the long-term trend of the market is up.

3. Trade plan.

First, identify your objective in investing. Next, set up a simple trade plan to start, and then set up a schedule, e.g. when to review market risk and when to trade. For casual investors, it could be a quarterly task. Excessive (such as everyday) checking our portfolios is a waste of time for most.

Following a trade plan consistently forces you to be disciplined in investing. You should stick with the strategies that have been proven and avoid the bad human nature such as greed, fears and ignorance.

This book could be part of a trade plan as a source for reference.

4. Match the ideas of this book to the current market conditions and your personal objectives and risk tolerance.

The market changes often and it is not always rational. Every one's investing objective is different. Even couch potatoes can benefit from this book by reading the chapters selected in Introduction.

5. Risk tolerance.

My objective is to make a decent return at the least risk and conserving of what I have is more important. Be a turtle investor who makes small but consistent profits. Many including many smartest people make millions but lose it all. Avoid options, leverages and margins. The exception is for well-off investors and / or during early recovery.

Customize your investing strategy depending on your risk tolerance. I describe mine here.

I am a retiree with enough money to have a comfortable living and hopefully it will stay this way. My strategy is conservative. However, life will be no fun if I just buy CDs and treasury bills (so is losing money in reckless investing). I do not want to take any risk for the sake of selling books or boosting my personal prestige. Here are my three major accounts.

1. Ultra conservative. I keep more cash in this account than the other two accounts. I do practice the strategy of 'all in' only in the Early Recovery stage of the market cycle. Most other time, I have cash, stocks with high values or sometimes some contra ETFs to lower my market risk.

2. Swing accounts. Buy deeply-valued stocks, and replace them with growth stocks during the Up and Peak stages of the market cycle. I am conservative in the Peak stage of the market cycle with stop loss. The average holding period is 6 months and longer for consideration on long-term capital gain tax.

3. Momentum accounts (most in Roth IRAs). However, switch at least some stocks to contra ETFs when the market is risky (temporary dips or the Bottom phase of the market cycle). The average holding period is one month.

6. Evaluate your requirements and apply what makes sense.

Every one's requirements are different and my investing style may be different from yours. Write down your risk tolerance, your time available for investing and your general knowledge (and your desire to learn investing). Only apply those ideas that make sense and fit your requirements.

If you are a beginner in investing, learn from this book and other basic books. Trade on paper. Buy stocks starting small. Believe in due diligence. Luck in investing only works short term.

For the intermediate investors, it is better to invest on mutual funds and ETFs. Master market timing before selecting individual stocks.

7. Be politically neutral in making investment decisions.

A political statement often offends a lot of folks. Do not let political bias distort your investment decisions. When I made political remarks on any party, I could be 100% right or 100% wrong to you according to which party you belong to.

Also do not let your bias cover your eyes in investing except to be socially responsible. To illustrate, do not let your religious belief to bar you from investing in stem cell technology.

Do not buy your company's stock solely because you work there. Do not be overconfident as the market is not always rational.

8. Trade effectively and monitor your trades.

9. Investing is multi discipline.

Investing requires knowledge in finance, accounting, economy, psychology, probability, statistics, PC skills, politics and government… This book touches many areas in basic terms.

10. Best strategy.

The best strategy is not to lose big money. Refer the chapter on Spotting Big Plunges. Try to identify Early Recovery phase of the market cycle and invest more aggressively in this phase.

In other phases of the market cycle, choose one of the following strategies depending on your skill, time and risk tolerance.

1. Conservative strategy. Remain more in cash all the time except during Early Recovery phase.

2. Less conservative. Buy Low and Sell High.

3. More aggressive. Besides 'Buy Low and Sell High', add 'Buy High and Sell Higher' to a small extend.

In any case, do not gamble the money you cannot afford to lose and check how risky is the current market. Do not bet your farm in any prediction even if you have a good record in predictions. One bad one could wipe out your entire savings.

This book provides you with a lot of knowledge in investing. However, you have to apply the ideas to the current market conditions and practice them.

When one strategy works consistently, stick with it. Limit your investing strategies to a few (one is fine) depending on your time and your objective.

11. Be socially responsible.

This book is my contribution to the marvelous country that allowed me to prosper and lead a comfortable life. Avoid defense companies, tobacco companies, etc.

12. After the holding period (6 months or less).

Analyze the bought stocks. If the fundamental metrics are worse than before and/or the outlook of the company, the sector and the company is changing for the worst, sell the stock.

Disclaimer: Do not gamble money that you cannot afford to lose. Past performance is a guideline and does not guarantee future performance.

Before and after insider trading

What happen before the insider purchases and after?

Before

To illustrate, a new drug is the final clinical trial. Bad result has been leaked (intentionally or unintentionally) and then the stock plunges. Suddenly, the stock price is up 10% with heavy volume as indicated by the charts (Chapter 15-17). What really happened is that the insiders know good or bad the results from the trial are. They may spread the rumor that the result is bad. Illegally his/her family members and friends buy the stock and it explains the surge of the stock price; SEC, take notice. Then insiders file the information of buying the stock themselves. Our website passes this info to us.

The point is the chart could be a better indicator than insider purchase and it happens before the purchase. If so, use insider purchase to confirm your evaluation.

After

From my limited test, I do not see any difference in annualized return for holding the stock for 3, 6 and even a year. I would sell my stock for the following reasons:

- when they reach my targeted prices,
- the fundamentals deteriorate or
- I need cash for the next buy.

I suspect the following happens. The big boys (fund managers...) are following the insiders and boost the stock price to a higher level if some nice developments turn out to be profitable. This can be identified by many websites including GuruFocus.com. The retail investors are coming in next. The stock price could be up further after earnings announcement if the development brings in extra profits and sales. After a year or two, most stock prices return to the average value.

Bonus: Simple Techniques
For starters, just trade ETFs such as SPY (an ETF simulating the market), and you can skip the rest of the book. It only takes a few minutes every month. When the market is not plunging, buy or keep SPY (or any ETF that stimulates the market); otherwise sell it. Do the opposite when the market is recovering.

If you have less than $50,000 to invest, just buy ETFs. Improve your investing skills by reading investment articles from this book and your broker's website. For example, Fidelity has a lot of information for investors.

Subscription to AAII is recommended. When your portfolio grows more than $50,000, invest on a subscription such as Value Line, GuruFocus, Zacks or IBD (more for momentum traders). Initially, use the information for paper trading on value stocks, which is usually available from brokers.

For the long term, knowledge is most important in your investing life and experience comes next. Retail investors have a lot of advantages over fund managers. However, I advise you NOT to be a trader. Hence, you should ignore the 'fabulous' trade systems that claim to be very profitable. Statistically most amateur traders lose money as they cannot compete with experienced, disciplined traders.

How to start
I recommend trading ETFs first and when the market is not risky. The very basic terms such as ETF are not fully explained here; try Investopedia for terms you need to know. Otherwise, this book would be doubled in size and it would bore most readers. Investopedia, your broker's website (especially Fidelity) and AAII (requiring subscription) provide many excellent articles. Alternatively, buy a book for beginners. Here are some freebies:

Click here for Morningstar classroom.
http://morningstar.com/cover/classroom.html
Click here for Vanguard.
https://investor.vanguard.com/investing/investor-education
Click here for Investopedia's Tutorials.
http://www.investopedia.com/university/
Click here for Yahoo!
http://finance.yahoo.com/education/begin_investing
Click here for Fidelity basic in investing.
https://www.fidelity.com/investment-guidance/investing-basics

1   Simplest market timing

Why market timing
Before 2000, market timing was a waste of time. However, after that, we have had two market plunges with the average loss of about 45%. It sounds harder to time the market than it actually is. We have a simple technique to detect market plunges and when to reenter the market. Our objective is reducing the loss to 25%.

Market timing depends on charts; the following describes how to use chart information without creating charts. Most charts will not identify the peaks and bottoms of the market as they depend on data (i.e., the stock prices). However, it would reduce further losses. It is simpler than it sounds. Just follow the procedure below.

The first part of this technique detects potential market plunges, and the second part advises you when to start reentering the market. It applies to individual stocks too. It also works to detect the trend of a sector (entering an ETF for the specific sector instead of SPY) and a specific stock.

Step-by-step procedure
When the market timer indicator (Death Cross) described next tells you to exit the market, sell SPY (an ETF simulating S&P 500). Do not forget to buy back SPY or similar ETF such as RSP, when the indicator (Golden Cross) tells you to return.

My experiences in 2000s
Basically I did the same as the above with some adaptations. I worked for a mutual fund company and they did not allow me to trade stocks effectively. However, I was allowed to trade sector funds offered by the company. Every two months, I switched to the sectors with the best performances for the last month. When most sectors were down for the last month, I rotated them to the money market fund. In March or April, 2000, I switched to traditional sectors from high-tech sectors (better to switch to market money fund). During the time, I bought those stocks that had cash enough to last more than two years judging by their burn rates. The indicators should do a better job.

How to detect market plunges without charts (similar to **Death Cross**)
1.   Bring up Finviz.com.

2. Enter SPY (or any ETF that simulates the market) or RSP for equally weighed SPY.
3. If SMA-200% is positive, it indicates that the market plunge has not been detected and you can skip the following steps.
4. The market is plunging if SMA-50% is more negative than SMA-200%. To illustrate this condition, SMA-200% is -2% and SMA-50% is -5%.
5. Conservative investors should sell most stocks starting with the riskiest ones first such as the ones with negative earnings, high P/Es and/or high Debt/Equity. Obtain this info from Finviz.com by entering the symbol of the stock you own.
6. Aggressive investors should sell all stocks. Extremely aggressive investors should sell all stocks, buy contra ETFs, and even short stocks. I do not recommend beginners to be aggressive.

Example
As of 2/12/2022, the following are from Finviz.com.

ETF	SMA-200	SMA-50	SMA-20	Death Cross?
SPY	-0.8%	-4.2%	-1.7%	Yes (Step #4)
RSP	-0.5%	-1.9%	0.4%	Yes (Step #4)

Both ETFs indicate the market is a confirmed crash from my indications using a technique similar to Death Cross. However, they are quite close, and we should keep an eye on these numbers. In this case, SMA-20 has not been used. If it is a false alarm, the Golden Cross would indicate it and you should return to equity; it could be quite common in volatile markets. The futures indicate that on Monday (2/14/22) the market would plunge further.

Another test is using SMA-350: When the current price is below SMA-300, it is a crash. SMA-20 has to be more negative than SMA-50 and it has not been used here.

When to return to the market (similar to Golden Cross)

Use the above in a reversed sense to detect whether the market has been recovering. However, when the SMA-200% turns positive, I would start buying value stocks (low P/E but the 'E' has to be positive, and/or low Debt/Equity).

1. Bring up Finviz.com.
2. Enter SPY (or any ETF that simulates the market).
3. If SMA-200% is negative, the market is not recovering, and you can skip the following steps.
4. Sell all contra ETFs and close all shorts if you have any.

5. Market recovery is confirmed when SMA-50% is more positive than SMA-200%. To illustrate this condition, SMA-200% is 2% and SMA-50% is 5%. Commit a large percent of cash (or all cash for aggressive investors) to stocks. If you do not know what to buy, buy SPY or an ETF that simulates the market.

How often should you check the market timing indicators?

Do the above once a month. When the SPY price is closer to SMA actions percentage, perform the above once a week. The charts and data for market timing described in this book are based on SMA-350 (Simple Moving Average) that is more preferable than this simple procedure, but it requires some simple charting.

Nothing is perfect

If the market timing is perfect, there would be no poor folks. The major 'defects' are:
- It does not detect the peak / bottom as it depends on past data. However, it would save you a lot during the crash.
- It is hard to determine whether it is a correction or a crash.
- From 2000 to 2010, there was only one false signal. The indicator tells you to exit and then tells you to reenter the market shortly. In most cases, you do not lose a lot. After 2010, we have more false signals.
- The market may not be rational or may be influenced due to specific conditions such as excessive printing of USD. If you do not mind charting, use SMA 350 (or 400) using SPY. Buy when the price is above SMA-350 (or SMA-400), and sell otherwise. SMA-400 reduces the number of false signals, but it is not nimble.

#Filler: Glad to be an investor

After watching the following YouTube video, I am glad my parents did not push me to play piano and also glad I do not have any musical gene. How can I compete with this kid?

https://www.youtube.com/watch?v=yf0B4rVoq44

Also, glad not into some life-threatening professions such as surgical doctors, soldiers, fire fighters, etc. I can make mistakes in investing from time to time without suffering from the consequences. With the uptrend market for most of the last 50 years, most investors should make good money. Thank God.

2   Quick analysis of ETFs

Evaluate an ETF

ETFs are a basket of stocks according to the market, a specific sector, country or a specific theme.

Yahoo!Finance used to give the P/E of an ETF. Try to get it from ETFdb.com. Enter the symbol of the ETF such as XLU, and then select Valuation. If it is below 15 and above zero, it could be a value ETF. Also, if the current price is lower than its NAV, it is sold at a discount (or premium vice versa). Compare its YTD Return to SPY's.

Alternatively, get similar info from http://www.multpl.com/. In addition, this website provides the following metrics: Shiller P/E, Price/Sales, and Price/Book.

From Finviz.com, enter the ETF symbol. If SMA-20%, SMA-50% and SMA-200% are all positive, most likely the ETF is in an uptrend. To illustrate, SMA-200 is Simple Moving Average for the last 200 trading sessions (no trading on weekends and specific holidays). The percent is how much the stock price of the ETF is above the SMA. If the percent is negative, it means the stock price is below the SMA.

If your average holding period of your stocks is about 50 days, SMA-50% is more appropriate to you.

If RSI(14) > 65, it is probably oversold; if it is < 30, it is probably under-sold (indicating value).

In addition, ensure the ETF's average volume is high (I suggest more than 10,000 shares), the market cap is more than 300 M, and it has low fees. Most popular ETFs have these characteristics. Beginners should avoid leveraged ETFs.

How to determine if the sector has been recovered

It is easier to profit by following the uptrend of an ETF using the above info. It is hard to detect when the bottom of an ETF has been reached. If SMA-20%, SMA-50% and SMA-200% are all positive, most likely the ETF is in an uptrend or it has recovered. It does not always happen as predicted, so use stops to protect your investment.

An example

First, determine whether the market is risky. Most beginners should not invest in a risky market. Advanced investors can bet against the market or a specific sector by buying contra ETFs or puts.

Next, you want to limit the number of sector ETFs by selecting those that are either in an uptrend or hitting bottom (bottom is hard to predict). Personally, I prefer sectors with long-term uptrends (indicated by articles found in many websites including cnnfn.com and Seeking Alpha.

For illustration purposes only for deteriorating market conditions, I would select the following ETFs: SPY (simulating the market based on large companies) and XLP (consumer staples). XLP should perform better than XLY (consumer discretionary) during a recession as those products are the necessities.

Technical indicators such as SMA-50 (Simple Moving Average for the last 50 sessions), SMA-200 and RSI(14) are obtained from Finviz.com and the rest are obtained from Yahoo!Finance.com. After you buy the ETF, use a stop loss to protect your investment. For example, biotech sector moved up for many months until it crashed in 2015. Change the stop loss value every month to protect your gains in this case.

As of 2/5/2016	SPY	XLP (staples)	XLY (discreet.)
Price	190	50	71
NAV	192	50	73
• **Technical**			
SMA-50	-4%	0%	-7%
SMA-200	-6%	2%	-7%
RSI(14)	44	50	36
Other	Double bottom at $186		
• **Fundamental**			
P/E	17	20	19
Yield	2.1%	2.5%	1.5%
YTD return	-5%	0.5%	-5%
Net asset	174 B	9 B	10 B

Explanation

- The figures may not be identical among websites due to the dates they are using.
- XLY has the best discount among the 3 ETFs as most investors believe a recession is coming.
- XLP has less down trend among the 3 ETFs as expected.
- XLY is more undersold among the three as expected.
- Double bottom is a technical pattern that indicates the stock would surge upward.
- SPY has a better value according to its P/E.
- XLY's dividend is the least among the three as they have more tech companies in the ETF. They have to plow back the profits to research and development.
- XLP has the best YTD return among the three.
- As long as the asset is above 500 M (200 M for specialized ETFs), it is fine and all three pass this mark.

There are many metrics such as Debt/Equity not readily available from most websites. Many sites list the top holdings of a specific ETF. Just average the metrics of the top ten or so of its stock holdings.

#Filler: Illogical logic

If we do not test for the pandemic, we would have zero increase in this pandemic. Some silly folks buy this argument. What happens to the once-great country?

Filler: The problems of the U.S.

1. Our political system. We waste time arguing between the two parties. There is no long-term planning, as the other party could claim the credit. Same as corporations' CEOs who care about their yearly bonuses.
2. The politicians have to satisfy their voters. Today give them free cash by jacking up the printing press. And ignore the long-term consequences.
3. We have to protect our workers, our environment... Hence, we cannot compete with many countries.
4. We have spent too much on the military and ignore our crumbling infrastructure.
5. Historically no country can rule the world forever.
6. We blame China, but ignore how hard-working Chinese are.

An example

This example evaluates RING, a gold miner, using ETFdb and Finviz that are free from the web. The data is from July, 6, 2020.

Bring up ETFdb and enter RING in the search. There is basic info that are important to me: Sector (gold miners), Asset Size (Large-Cap), Issuer (iShares), Inception (Jan. 31, 2012), Expense Ratio (0.39%) and Tax Form (1099).

They fit all my requirements. The expense ratio is higher than most ETFs that simulate an index such as SPY. I try to trade ETFs using Tax Form 1099 in my taxable accounts. The large cap created about 8 years ago by a reputable company is good.

Select "Dividend and Valuation". P/E of 17.39 is fine in a rank of 11 in 27 in a similar group of ETFs. As in my books, I stated it is hard to evaluate miners. I buy this ETF primarily to fight the possibility of inflation and the potential depreciation of USD. The dividend rate of 0.52% (0.70% from Finviz) is in the low range of the scale; it is fine for me as dividend is not my concern.

There is more info from this website. For simplicity, bring up Finviz:
- The short-term trend is up (SMA-20% = 8% and SMA-50% = 7%).
- The long-term trend is up (SMA-200% = 26%).
- It is close to overbought (RSI(14) = 64%; 65% to me is overbought).
- It is -4% from 52-w High. It has performed well from the YTD, Last Year, Last Quarter, Last Month and Last Week.
- It almost doubled in price from mid-March this year.
- Avg. Vol. is fine.

From ETFdb, check the Holding. It has 39 stocks, so it is quite diversified for this industry. The two top holdings are NEM (19%) and ABX (18%), which is listed as GOLD in NYSX. I also consider buying these two stocks in addition to RING. You can estimate the other metrics that are not available by averaging these two stocks. Here is my summary:

STOCK	NEM	GOLD
Forward P/E	20	25
Debt / Share	0.31	0.24
ROE	17%	22%
Sales Q/Q	43%	30%
EPS Q/Q	389%	254%
SMA50	2%	4%
RSI(14)	59%	60%
Insider Trans	-13%	N/A
Fidelity's Equity Summary Score	6.1	6.8

3   Rotate four ETFs

We can beat the market by rotating one ETF that represents the market such as SPY and cash via market timing. Aggressive investors can add SH or PSQ (contra ETFs) to the four to have better returns during market plunges.

During a market uptrend, rotating the following four ETFs could be more profitable than staying with SPY (or any ETF that simulates the market). Be warned that a short-term capital gain in taxable accounts is not treated as favorably as the long-term capital gain; check current tax laws.

The allocation percentages depend on your individual risk tolerance. You can use indexed mutual funds. Compare their expenses and restrictions. Some mutual funds charge you if you withdraw within a specific time period.

Select the best performer of last month (from Seeking Alpha, cnnFn, or one of many ETF/mutual fund sites). Add a contra ETF such as SH to take advantage of a falling market for more aggressive investors. Add sector ETFs to the described four ETFs such as XLY, XLP, XLE, XLF, XLU, IYW, XHB, IYM, OIL and XLU to expand your selection.

ETFs	Money Market	U.S.	International	Bond
Fidelity		Spartan Total Market	Spartan Global Market	Spartan US Bond
Vanguard		Total Stock Market	Total International Market	Total Bond Market
My choice	Fidelity	SPY	Vanguard	Fidelity
Suggest %				
During Market plunge	90%	0%	0%	10%
After plunge	10%	60%	20%	10%

Explanation

- The above are suggestions only. If your broker offers similar ETFs, consider using them.
- Check out any restrictions of the ETFs and commissions.
- 4 ETFs (one actually is a money market fund) are enough for most starters. They are diversified, low-cost and you do not need rebalancing except during a market plunge.
- The percentages are suggestions only. If you are less risk tolerant, allocate more to a money market fund, CD and/or bond ETF.
- Have at least 10% allocated to the money market fund for safety.
- When the market is risky, reduce stock equities (i.e., increase money market and bond allocations).
- The symbols for Fidelity ETFs are FSTMX, FSGDX and FBIDX.
- The symbols for Vanguard ETFs are VTSMX, VGTSX and VBMFX.
- If you are more advanced, use additional sector ETFs to rotate. Also buy long-term bond funds (such as 30-year Treasury) when the interest rate is 10% or more.

#Filler: Where common sense is not common sense

Excessive printing of money is not a long-term solution. Servicing the huge debt weakens our competitiveness. The politicians just want to buy votes today and finance their campaigns. Our next generations have to pay for these huge debts.

#Filler: Cayman Island

Most global corporations are making fun of our tax system. Moving the "headquarter" to low-tax countries such as Cayman Island with a mailbox, a bank account and/or an office that has never been used is a norm. The profitable Boeing has negative tax liability. What a shame!

4   Simplest ways to evaluate stocks

Beginners should trade ETFs only. This chapter is for the readers who are ready or getting ready to trade stocks. In general, ETFs are diversified, less volatile than trading stocks. However, stocks offer higher profit but higher risk.

Many stock researches have already been done recently and some are available free of charge. I have no affiliation with Fidelity except I retired from it. You can open an account with them with no balance. Their Equity Summary Score is one of the best indicators; I check out **value** stocks with scores higher than 8. Concentrate on fundamental metrics such as P/E for long-term holds, and momentum metrics for short-term holds. Add criteria to limit the number of screened stocks. Finviz.com is a free screener.

Several sources

The popular ones are Morningstar, Value Line, The Street and Zacks (currently free for rankings of individual stocks). If they are not free, check out whether they are available from your local library. I have 3 simple ways to evaluate stocks starting with the simplest. In addition, read the articles on the selected stocks from Fidelity, Finviz, Seeking Alpha and many other sources for further evaluation.

Fidelity

Select only stocks that have Fidelity's Equity Summary Score 8 or higher. There are tons of information about a stock. Once in a while I did not agree with this score such as SHOP and ZM that scored high in August, 2020. Include the following for your analysis.

A modified stock selection based on a magazine article

Most metrics are available from Finviz except EV/EBITDA.

1. Forward P/E (expected earnings and not based on the last twelve months). It should range from 5 to 15 (10 to 25 for high tech stocks). EV/EBITDA (from Yahoo!Finance) is a better choice as it includes the debts and cash than P/E; it would be more effective if it uses forward earnings. If you do not use EV/EBITDA, ensure Debt/Equity is less than 0.5 except for the debt-intensive industries.

2. ROE (Return of Equity) measures how well the company uses the capital. I prefer stocks with ROE greater than 5%.

3. Volatility. Conservative investors should select stocks with a beta of less than one (i.e., less volatile).

4. Insider Transactions for sales (i.e., negative) should be less than 5%. If it is -5%, most likely the insiders are dumping it.

5. Compare the metrics such as P/E and Debt/Equity to its five-year average and its competitors (available in Fidelity).

6. Momentum. Check out the SMA-50 (actually SMA-50%) and SMA-200. Ideally, they should be positive. SMA-50% is especially important for stocks you do not want to keep for a long time.

7. Check out articles on the stock as some recent events (for example a new lawsuit) have not been included in the metrics.

8. Compare the trend of the sector this stock is in. Under Finviz, enter the related sector ETF.

Summary

The sources are Fidelity (Equity Summary Score and various comparisons), Finviz and Yahoo!Finance (for EV/EBITDA). Value stocks should be held longer.

Category	Score / Metric	Value /Momentum
Score	Fidelity's Equity Summary Score	Both
Value	EV/EBITDA	Value
	P/E cheaper compared to 5-year avg.	Value
	P/E cheaper compared to its sector.	Value
	Insider Purchases	Both
Safety	Debt/Equity	Value
	Compare it to its sector.	Value
Momentum	50-SMA%	Momentum

	200-SMA% (for long term holds).	Value
Articles	Check out latest events	Both
Market	No purchase if market is risky.	Momentum

A simple scoring system using Finviz

Bring up Finviz.com and then enter the stock symbol.

No.	Metric	Good	Bad	Score
1	Forward P/E[1]	Between 2.5 and 12.5, Score = 2	> 50 or < 0, Score = -1	
2	P/ FCF[1]	< 12, Score = 1	>30 or < 0, Score = -1	
3	P/S[1]	< 0.8, Score = 1	< 0, Score = -1	
4	P/ B[1]	< 1, Score = 1	< 0, Score = -1	
	Compare quarter to quarter of last year			
5	Sales Q/Q	> 15%, Score = 1	< 0, Score = -1	
6	EPS Q/Q	> 20%, Score = 1	< 0, Score = -1	
			Grand Score	
	Stock Symbol Date[2]	Current Price	SPY	

Footnote

[1] Negative values for Sales (due to accounting adjustments), Equity and Book are possible but not likely.

[2] The last row is for your information only. SPY is used to measure whether it will beat the market by comparing the return of this stock to the return of SPY.

The Score

Score each metric and sum up all the scores giving the Grand Score. If the Grand Score is 3, the stock passes this scoring system. Even if it is a 2, it still deserves further analysis if you have time. You may want to add scores from other vendors. To illustrate on using Fidelity, add 1 to the score if Fidelity's Equity Summary score is 8 or higher. Monitor the performance after every 6 months or so to see whether this scoring system beats the market.

Very basic advice for beginners

Beginners should stick with U.S. stocks with Market Cap greater than 800 M (million), Debt/Equity less than .25 (25%) except for debt-intensive industries such as utilities and airlines and Forward P/E between 5 to 20 (25 for high-tech companies). These metrics are all available from Finviz.com, which is free.

Do not have more than 20% of your portfolio in one stock (unless it is an ETF or mutual fund) and do not have more than 30% of your portfolio in one sector.

For more conservative investors, buy non-volatile stocks whose beta (available from Yahoo!Finance) is less than 1. Beta of 1 represents the market (the S&P 500 index). For example, a stock with beta 1.5 statistically fluctuates more than 50% of the market and hence it is very volatile.

Try paper trading to check out your strategy and your skill in trading stocks. If your broker does not provide one, use a spreadsheet to record your trades or check the availability of simulator.investopedia.com.

#Filler: Silence is golden

I am glad I did not give advice to a friend who had to decide whether to take a lump sum payment or an annuity. The correction in March, 2020 would wipe out a lot of his portfolio if he took the lump sum payment. No one would share his profits when the predictions are correct, but the blame if it does not materialize.

It is the same in investing that nothing is certain. With educated guesses, we should have more rights than wrongs especially in the long run.

5 Simplest technical analysis

When the stock, the sector that the stock is in and the market are all above its SMA-N averages (Single Moving Average for the last N sessions), most likely the stock is trending up.

1. Bring up Finviz.com from your browser.

2. Enter SPY. Write down the SMA-200 (Single Moving Average for 200 sessions). Positive numbers indicate that the trend for the market is up.

   However, the market could be peaking or overbought. Be careful when SMA-200 is over 5% and / or RSI(14) is over 65%. RSI is a metric on overbought / underbought.

3. Enter the sector ETF the stock is in. Write down the SMA-50. Positive numbers indicate that trend for the sector is up.

   However, the sector could be peaking or overbought. Be careful when the SMA-200 is over 10% and / or RSI(14) is over 65%.

4. Enter the stock symbol. If your average holding period of the stocks is 200, use SMA-200 and so on. I recommend SMA-200 for holding value stocks long term and SMA-50 for momentum stocks. Write down the SMA-N for your stock. Positive numbers indicate that the trend is up.

   However, the stock could be peaking or overbought. Be careful when the SMA-200 (or SMA-50) is over 25% and / or RSI(14) is over 65%.

If the above three criteria and the fundamental criteria are satisfied, most likely it is a good buy. If you buy sector ETFs or mutual funds only, you can skip step #4. In any case, use stop loss to protect your investment.

#Filler: The Ten Commandments of Investing.
http://www.investopedia.com/articles/basics/07/10commandments.asp

- Set goals. * Personal finances in order. * Ask questions. * Do not follow the herd. * Due diligence. * Be humble. * Be patient. * Be moderate. * No unnecessary churning. * Be safe. * Do not follow blindly.
- My additions: * Diversify. * Study market timing. * Protect your losses and profits. * Monitor your screens and your metrics. * Be emotionally detached from investments. * Learn from mistakes. * Stay away from bubbles. * Be socially responsible.

6   The best strategy

The best-kept secret in investing is to buy a weighed ETF. I use SPY as an example here. This ETF is well diversified as it keeps all 500 stocks in the S&P 500 index. The ETF has a higher position (in percentage) on stocks with higher market cap. The stocks with higher market caps usually grow the market cap by having good management and good products. The bad stocks are deleted from the index periodically.

The second best-kept secret is using simple market timing as described in this book to reduce the losses in market crashes.

It is very hard to beat this strategy. You do not need any knowledge in investing, and you only spend a few minutes every month to time the market. The market is risky when the metrics show you so such as the price is close to the simple moving average in using SMA-350 method; in this case you time the market more frequently.

7   Don'ts for beginners

- Do not use leverage: options, margin and leveraged ETFs.
- Do not short stocks.
- Buy low and sell high.
- Buy value stocks. Sell profitable stocks after a year and losers before holding 12 months for favorable tax treatments in non-retirement accounts. Be a turtle investor.
- Limit momentum trades.
- Use stops to protect your portfolio.
- Do not follow 'experts' blindly (most have their own agenda).
- Do not trade penny stocks (i.e., stocks less than 200 M and/or price less than $1 to my definitions).
- Venture into momentum trading when you have knowledge and time. Avoid trading systems that are available.
- Do not day trade. Most beginners lose most of their money.
- Do not take classes / seminars that promise you big money - if it works, they will give out their secrets.
- Be selective on investing subscriptions. If they give you a handful of stocks to thousands of subscribers, most likely the actual performance will not be good. Check their past performances that use real money.

8   Summary

The following improves the odds of success but there is no guarantee.

Risky Market?
Bring up Finviz.com. Enter SPY. If both SMA-50% and SMA-200% are both negative, do not invest especially when SMA-50% is more negative than SMA-200%.

Evaluate value stocks from others' researches
Gather a list of stocks from screens and/or recommendations from magazines. Use researches that are free. Value stocks should be kept for at least 6 months. In six months or so, evaluate the bought stocks again to see whether you want to sell the stocks. Some other sites may provide free trial or one-time evaluation: IBD, GuruFocus, Zacks and Morningstar. Fidelity requires an account but there is no minimum position.

Name	Pass Grade	Link
Fidelity's Equity Summary Score	>=8	
Value Line[2]	Timeliness > Average	
	Proj. 3-5 yr.% > 5%	
VectorVest[1]	VST > 1 and RV > 1	Link

[1]   Should be available from your local library.

[2]   Free for limited number of stocks and free trial.

Evaluate stocks
Bring up Finviz.com and enter the stock symbol.

Metric	Passing Grade
Forward P/E	Between 5 and 20 (25 for tech stocks)
P/FCF	< 15 and ratio is positive
Sales Q/Q	>10
EPS Q/Q	>15

Intangible Analysis
Bring up Finviz, Fidelity, Yahoo!Finance or Seeking Alpha (fewer articles now) and enter the stock symbol. To prevent manipulation, the stocks

should have larger cap (> 200 M) and higher daily average volume (> 10,000 shares).

Bonus: Investing for 'lazy' folks

You have better things to do than investing or you do not have the time, the desire to learn and/or expertise in investing. You should be better off to buy ETFs.

I recommend the following 4 ETFs. If you have $100,000 to invest, buy $25,000 for each recommended ETF. Consult your financial advisor before taking any action. The recommended ETFs should have a large market cap (the ETFs themselves and not the stocks they hold) and have a high volume.

Most returns started on July 1 and ended on July 1 the following year; this article is written on July 20, 2021. All are annualized returns for easy comparison. Fees, commissions and dividends have not been included; you can add the dividend yield and prorate it for YTD return.

Symbol	Name	YTD[1] Return	1 Year[2]	5 Years[3]	Bear[4]
IWF	Russel 1000G	30%	34%	40%	-33%
QQQ	QQQ	30%	46%	42%	-31%
VTI	Vang. Viper Tot	34%	22%	42%	-35%
VUG	Vang. Growth	37%	33%	41%	-32%
Avg.		31%	34%	41%	-33%
SPY[5]		34%	21%	39%	-35%
Beat[6]		-9%	60%	6%	7%

[1] The start date is 1/4/2021 and the end date is 7/1/2021.
[2] The start date is 7/1/2020 and the end date is 7/1/2021.
[3] The start date is 7/1/2016 and the end date is 7/1/2021.
[4] The start date is 1/2/2008 and the end date is 4/1/2009. My estimates.
[5] SPY is the ETF for the S&P 500 index. It is used as a yardstick.
[6] = (Avg. − SPY) / SPY. Again, it does not include fees, commissions and dividends.

Comments:

- The YTD is the only period that this portfolio does not beat SPY (the market to many). It could mean the market could be changing the favorite from growth stocks to value stocks. However, 31% return is far above the average of the market.
- The one-year return beats the market by 60%.
- The 5-year return beats SPY only by 6%, but the return of 41% is nothing to sneeze at.
- All except Vanguard's Viper Total are ETFs for growth stocks. Hence, I expected it would not beat the market, but it still did by 7%.
- You can time the market using the techniques described in this book as often as you can. When the indicator tells you to exit, you can sell these ETFs and reenter the market when it recovers. Riskier investors can buy contra ETFs such as PSQ and SH instead of holding cash when the market is down.
- At least once in a year review the selection. Use ETFdb.com for information. If you do not have time, it is fine skipping the review. When you switch ETFs, taxes should be considered.
- Most ETFs replace some stocks periodically to ensure better appreciation potential.

Bonus: Sample portfolio

It is a suggested sample. You need to tailor it to fit your personal requirements and your risk tolerance. In general, you should have an emergency fund for at least 3 months (6 months preferred). Many of our generation have one or even no layoff. However, I estimate the current generation will have 3 layoffs in their work life. It is due to automation, artificial intelligence, global economy, etc.

The rough estimate of stock holding in distribution between stock and bond is equal to 100 – Your Age. To illustrate in the following three portfolios, I use a 30-year-old, and hence he should have 70% in stocks and 30% in bonds (including gold, CDs and cash).

In addition, some sectors are better than others according to the market conditions. The following three portfolios are for regular, todays' market and one during a market crash. I use low-cost ETFs exclusively. ETF is exchange-traded funds. They are traded similar to stocks, but most are more diversified; their fees are usually lower than mutual funds.

ETF	Normal	Today (2/2021)	Crashing[5]
SPY[1]	40%	30%	0%
QQQ[2]	5%	10%	0%
ARKK[2]	5%	0%	0%
VTIAX[3]	20%	5%	0%
LQD[3]	15%	20%	5%
GLD	5%	15%	15%
CD	5%	0%	0%
Cash	5%	20%	60%[6]
SH[4]	0%	0%	5%
PSQ[4]	0%	0%	15%

[1] VOO is a low-fee alternative for SPY.

[2] QQQ has more tech stocks, while ARKK is an actively managed ETF specializing in 'disruptive technologies'. During market crashes, avoid them, esp. ARKK.

[3] VTIAX is an ETF for global companies. LQD is an ETF for corporate bonds.

[4] SH and PSQ are contra ETF to SPY and QQQ. They are shorting the corresponding index. When the market is recovering, switch them back to SPY and QQQ.

[5] Need to balance the allocations about two times a year as ETFs can grow or shrink. When the market crashes, rebalance it right away. All markets will crash, and the last two (2000 and 2008) have an average loss of about 45%. Refer to the chapter "Simplest marketing timing".

[6] Today's low interest rate does not benefit us for CDs. I would leave the cash not invested and wait for the recovery to move back to stocks.

Of course, everyone's situation is different. If you are conservative, do not buy SH and PSQ. If you are afraid of inflation (especially due to the excessive printing of money), allocate more on GLD, a gold ETF.

Do not listen to financial news. They are used by institutional investors / analysts to manipulate the market. Many times they act the opposite from what they preach. This is the primary reason retail investors do not do better. With the GameStop incident, do not invest in most hedge funds. Buffett has proved the hedge funds with their high fees cannot buy an indexed ETF such as SPY.

The above is my recommendation. In the long run, it should work fine. Consult your financial advisor before taking actions. Most info is from RainIsHere, a Cantonese YouTuber.

#Filler: Simple measures to reduce net security.
Do not click any links from unknown sources. Some seem to be ok but not. MalwareBytes, for checking viruses, is free for download (they do not pay me).

Personally, I use a Chromebook for my financial transactions and a two-factor login for my stock trading.

#Filler "How to make a 50% return"

https://www.youtube.com/watch?v=eEto5nEkf1Y

#Filler Buffett, the person.
https://www.youtube.com/watch?v=w-eX4sZi-Zs

Epilogue

After my early retirement, I have been spending most of my time in investing, running thousands of simulation and reading over one hundred books in investing. Starting from 2000, I have been doing extraordinary good. I comment in financial blogs and save the good ones in my own blog, so I can refer them later on. After several years, I have enough information to write a book.

At first, I want to write a book for one reader only: Me. My children have better things to do than investing. I do not need to keep my 'secrets' for them. That's why I publish this book. From the version before its release, it had been doing better than my expectation. It has been very rewarding, when my readers tell me how much they enjoy and benefit from this book.

I do not believe that this book or any book is the Holy Grail in investing. However, it has a lot of fresh ideas and good pointers that have brought me financial success (at least so far). I ask my readers to challenge my pointers and ensure they are applicable in today's market and meet their objectives and requirements.

A good pointer can make you thousands of dollars, and a bad or misinterpreted one can do the opposite. Always do paper trading on any strategy and / or idea before you commit real money on it. Start your strategy with cash in small increments until you have more confidence.

Very seldom you want to buy another book from the same author. That's why I copied many chapters from Debunk the Myths in Investing to this book.

Hopefully, this book's primary objective enabling you to be a better investor is met

If you believe this book is beneficial, please comment in amazon.com or similar sites.

The next book follows this series is Scoring Stocks.

Appendix 1 – All my books

- Art of Investing (highly recommended combining most of my books on investing). It has over 500 pages (6*9), double the size of an average investing book. Similar books: Using Fidelity. Using Finviz.
- Sector Rotation: 21 Strategies, Strategies and Shorting Stocks and ETFs have more specific chapters on the topic.
- Using Profitable Investing Sites. Investing Lessons.
- Best stocks for 2022.
- "Nuclear War with China?"
- Books for today's market: Profit from Coming Market Crash.
- The following books are in a series: Finding Profitable Stocks, Market Timing and Scoring Stocks.
- Books on strategies: Trading System, Swing (Rotation + Momentum), ETF Rotation for Couch Potatoes, Momentum, SuperStocks, Dividend, Penny & Micro Stock, and Retiree.
- Books for advance beginners: Be an expert (highly recommended), Introduce, Investing for Beginners, Beat Fund Managers, Profit via ETFs, Buffett, Ideas, Conservative and Top-Down.
- Miscellaneous: Investing Strategies. Buy Low and Sell High. Buy High and sell Higher. Buffettology. Technical Analysis. Trading Stocks.
- Concise Editions and Introduction Editions are available at very low prices and are competitive with books of similar sizes (50 pages) and prices ($3 range).

Most books have paperbacks. Links and offers are subject to change without notice.

Best stocks to buy for 2022

We care about performance only. Not considering dividends and fees, my last three books in this series have beaten the SPY (the market to most) by **110%, 71% and 25%** from the publish date to 07/01/2021. Next book could be on 12/15/2022

Book	Stocks	Return	Ann.	Beat SPY by
Best Book for 2021 2nd Edition	10	20%	52%	110%
Best Book for 2021	4	29%	52%	71%
Best Book to Buy from Aug, 2020	14	42%	45%	25%
Avg.	9	31%	50%	69%

Sector Rotation: 21 Strategies

- On 5/26/2020, I searched for "Sector Rotation" under Amazon's Book. They are listed in the same order except my book Sector Rotation: 21 Strategies.

Book	Date	Size[1]	Kindle $[1]	Hard $
Sector Rotation: 21 Strategies	**05/2020**	**425**	**$9.95**	**$24.95**
Super Sectors	09/2010	289	$26.39	$49.95
Dual Momentum Investing	11/2014	240	$40.40	$42.20
Sector Investing	05/1996	260		$29.94
Sector Trading Strategies	08/2007	164	$26.39	$16.66
The Sector Strategist	03/2012	225	$26.39	$44.96
ETF Rotation	10/2012	125	$9.95	$14.99
Optimal… Sector Rotation	07/2015	80		$44.07

[1] From Amazon on size and prices as of 5/25/2020.

My book won in all categories except the price for hard copy in one. However, my book won as the lowest cost per page by a wide margin. In addition, as of 5/2020 I bet that no author besides me made over 4 times using sector rotation starting the amount more than his yearly salary then.

- I have **21** strategies in sector rotation while most books have only one. It ranges from simple rotation of a stock ETF and cash for beginners to many advanced strategies for experts. Most other books have one or two strategies.
- Andrew, a contributor on Sector Rotation article at Seeking Alpha, said, "Great stuff, Tony. It's great to meet experienced traders such as yourself. I had a browse through the book and think your method is a little more refined than mine."
- "You have written the book in a way that makes good and logical sense." Bill.
- Do not be fooled by past performances. Just check the recent performance of the top 50 stocks selected by IBD in the last five years. The mediocre result (hopefully it will change) could be due to too many followers and/or there is no evergreen strategy. I seldom heard the fantastic results from the followers of O'Neil, our greatest chartist. The adaptive strategy of this book shows you how to select the most profitable strategy for the current market.
- I switched most (if not all) my sector funds in April, 2000 from technology sectors to traditional sectors (better to money market fund). We can reduce losses by spotting market plunges and the sector trend.

Investing Strategies: Build, Monitor and Execute

It is similar book as Sector Rotation and Shorting Stocks (below), but concentrates in creating, monitoring and executing strategies.

Shorting Stocks and ETFs
Recent performances.

Stocks	Short Date	Close date	Duration	Return	Annualized
ACVA	06/10/21	09/29/21	111	22%	72%
CCL	07/14/21	09/29/21	77	-8%	-36%
CENX	09/17/21	09/29/21	12	3%	105%
CLOV	09/16/21	09/29/21	13	10%	291%
CSPR	09/16/21	09/29/21	13	33%	917%
EOSE	09/15/21	09/29/21	14	10%	261%
MILE	07/22/21	09/29/21	69	53%	279%
NCLH	07/27/21	09/29/21	64	-5%	-27%
REAL	06/04/21	09/29/21	117	22%	68%
UAVS	06/04/21	09/29/21	117	41%	127%
Average	07/30/21	09/29/21	61	18%	206%
RSP	S&P 500			0%	

It is for education purposes and I am not responsible for any errors. As in most parts of this book, commissions, dividends and fees (interest for shorts) are not included, and hence the returns are less than specified. They are real and all trades for the period.

Stocks	Short Date	Close date	Duration	Return	Annualized
BBIG[1]	09/30/21	11/19/21[1]	50	35%	258%
BFLY	09/30/21	11/18/21	49	14%	107%
EOLS	11/10/21	11/17/21	7	10%	523%
FLDM	10/13/21	11/18/21	36	14%	147%
MKFG	10/27/21	11/18/21	22	-9%	-149%
PAVM[1]	10/20/21	11/19/21[1]	30	34%	413%
TSP	10/05/21	11/18/21	44	-11%	-91%
VRM	10/13/21	11/17/21	35	13%	135%
Average	10/14/21	11/18/21	34	13%	168%
RSP	S&P 500			4%	

Appendix 2 – Art of Investing

Art of Investing consisting of 15 books in 1. Besides saving money and your digital shelve space, it gives you quick reference and concentration on the topic you're currently interested in. It covers most investing topics in investing excluding speculative investing such as currency trading and day trading. It has over 500 pages (6*9), about the size of two investing books of average size.

The 15 books

Book No.	Amazon.com
1	Simple techniques
2	Finding Stocks
3	Evaluating Stocks
4	Scoring Stocks
5	Trading Stocks
6	Market Timing
7	Strategies
8	Sector Rotation
9	Insider Trading
10	Penny Stocks & Micro Cap
11	Momentum Investing
12	Dividend Investing
13	Technical Analysis
14	Investing Ideas
15	Buffettology

The book links are subject to change without notice.

"How to be a billionaire" is for beginners and couch potatoes, who can use the advanced features of this book in the simplest and less time-consuming techniques. Most advance users can skip this section unless they want to use some of the short cuts described.

We start with the basic books Finding Stocks, Evaluate Stocks, Trading Stocks and Market Timing. You can select and start with one of the many styles and strategies in investing such as swing trading and top-down strategy. Many tools are described in other books such as ETFs, technical analysis, covered calls and trading plan.

Many books start with "Why" to lure you to read more and are followed by "How" and then the theory behind the book.
If the book you're reading is beneficial to you, imagine how it would with 850 pages.

\# Most readers' comments are on "Debunk the Myths in Investing", which this book is originally based on. As of 2018, I did not know any of the commentators on my books.

"I skipped ahead to his chapter book 14 (of "Complete the Art of Investing"), Investment Advice just to get a feel of his writing style. His research is phenomenal and doesn't overwhelm with big words or catchy "sales-like" tactics.

I truly believe this ordinary man, Mr. Tony Pow, has a gift of explaining his experience as an investor without the bull crap of trying to make you buy his stuff. He seemingly just wants to share his knowledge, tips, and clarity of definitions for the kind of folks like me who want to understand something FIRST before jumping in with emotions of trying to make a boat load of money. I like the technical analysis side he brings.

Mr. Tony Pow talks about hidden gems in his book; well....quite frankly, he is a hidden gem. Thank you and I will also post my comments about this author to my Facebook page!" – JB on this book.

"Excellent book, recommend to all investors… great knowledge. It has fine-tuned my investing strategies… Your book is hard to set aside, as I read it all the time learning good techniques and analysis of stocks, ETF… Since I purchased your book in March, I have underlined, highlighted and placed tabs on top of pages for quick reference." – Aileron on this book.

"Tony, I just finished reading your 2nd edition. It's my pleasure to report that I found it most interesting. You're welcome to use this blurb if you like:

Debunk the Myths in Investing is an all-encompassing look at not only the most salient factors influencing markets and investors, but also a from-the-trenches look at many of the misconceptions and mistakes too many investors make. Reading this book may save not only time and aggravation but money as well!"

Joseph Shaefer, CEO, Stanford Wealth Management LLC.

"Tony, Great work!" from James and Chris, who are portfolio managers.

"'Debunk the Myths in Investing' is a comprehensive book on investing that deals with many aspects of this tense profession in which with a lot of knowledge and a bit of luck (or vice versa) one can greatly benefit…

Therefore 'Debunk the Myths in Investing' is an interesting book that on its 500 pages offer a lot of knowledge related to investing world and many practical advice, so I can recommend its reading if you're interested in this topic."
- Denis Vukosav, Top 500 Reviewers at Amazon.com.

"490 pages (Debunk) of a genius's ranting and hypothesis with various theories throughout, written light-heartedly with ample doses of humor…Yes, the myth of not being able to profitably time the market is BUSTED…

One might ask… Why is he giving away the results of his hard-earned research for only $20? He states that his children are not interested in investing and wants to share his efforts with the world." - Abe Agoda.

"Excellent book, recommend to all investors… great knowledge. It has fine-tuned my investing strategies… Your book is hard to set aside, as I read it all the time learning good techniques and analysis of stocks, ETF… Since I purchased your book in March, I have underlined, highlighted and placed tabs on top of pages for quick reference." - Aileron on this book.

"Great stuff, Tony. It's great to meet experienced traders such as yourself. I had a browse through the book and think your method is a little more refined than mine."
"Your strategy is very rules based and solid. I sometimes envy people who have developed something like this."

Making 50% in one month
I claim to have the best one-month performance ever for recommending 8 or more stocks without using options and leverage. My following return is 57% in a month or 621% annualized. They are slightly different as I calculated the average from the averages of three different accounts. The average buy date is 12/26/18 and the "current date" is 01/28/19.

The performance may not be repeated. I will use the same screen for the coming years and even the expected 10% (or 120% annualized) is very good.

I used the same screen for searching stock candidates. I spent a total of about 20 hours from Dec. 15, 2018 to Jan. 5, 2019.

Stock	Buy Price	Sold or Current Price	Buy date	Sold or Current date	Profit %	Profit % Ann.	Status
CHK	2.13	2.99	01/03/09	01/18/19	40%	982%	Sold
MNK	16.41	21.45	01/03/19	01/25/19	31%	510%	Sold
MNK	16.43	21.45	01/03/19	01/25/19	31%	507%	Sold
NNBR	5.68	8.58	12/26/18	01/28/19	51%	565%	
NNBR	5.72	8.58	12/26/18	01/28/19	66%	727%	
ESTE	4.35	6.45	12/26/18	01/18/19	48%	766%	Sold
LCI	4.61	8.29	12/21/18	01/28/19	80%	767%	
MDR	8.01	9.13	01/08/19	01/28/19	14%	255%	
YRCW	3.29	5.78	12/21/18	01/28/19	76%	727%	
YRCW	3.26	5.78	12/21/18	01/28/19	77%	742%	
ASRT	3.56	4.18	12/26/18	01/28/19	17%	193%	
UTCC	7.13	11.00	12/26/18	01/28/19	54%	600%	
YRCW	2.92	5.78	12/26/18	01/28/19	98%	1083%	

Best one-year return
I claim to have the best-performed article in Seeking Alpha history, an investing site, for recommending 15 or more stocks in one year after the publish date without using options and leverage.

https://seekingalpha.com/article/1095671-amazing-returns-velti-alcatel-lucent-alpha-natural-resources

Your choice for your next book

I was surprised that one told me $25 is a lot for an investing book. It could be less than a taxi cab to the airport attending a seminar, and the time is peanut comparatively.

"Art of investing 2nd Edition" should be your first choice. If you are short-term trading, I recommend "Sector Rotation: 21 Strategies" and "Shorting Stocks /ETFs 2nd Edition". These books together with "Using Fidelity" and "Using Finviz" share many articles.

A new book every Dec. 15 with a July update (not a promise) is my selections on stocks. So far, the returns of the selected stocks are phenomenal. "A nuclear war with China?" is my views on politics.

Appendix 3 - Our window to the investing world

The paperback version of this chapter can be found in the following link.
http://ebmyth.blogspot.com/2013/11/web-sites.html

- **General**
  Wikipedia / Investopedia /Yahoo!Finance / MarketWatch / Cnnfn / Morningstar /CNBC / Bloomberg / WSJ / Barron's / Motley Fool / TheStreet
- **Evaluate stocks**
  Finviz / SeekingAlpha / MSN Money / Zacks / Daily Finance / ADR / Fidelity / Earnings Impact / OpenInsider / NYSE / NASDAQ / SEC / SEC for 10K and 10Q (quarterly) reports required to file for listed stocks in major exchanges.
- **Charts**
  BigCharts / FreeStockCharts / StockCharts /
- **Screens**
  Yahoo!Finance / Finviz / CNBC / Morningstar /
- **Besides stocks**
  123Jump / Hoover's Online / FINRA Bond Market Data / REIT / Commodity Futures / Option Industry
- **Vendors**
  AAII / Zacks / IBD / GuruFocus / VectorVest / Fidelity / Interactive Brokers / Merrill Lynch /
- **Economy.**
  Econday / EcoconStats / Federal Reserve / Economist /
- **Misc.**
  Dow Jones Indices / Russell / Wilshire / IRS / Wikinvest / ETF Database / ETF Trends / Nolo (estate planning) / AARP /

Appendix 4 - ETFs / Mutual Funds

What is an ETF

ETFs have basic differences from mutual funds: 1. Lower management expenses, 2. Trade ETFs same as stocks, and 3. Usually more diversified but not more selective than the related mutual funds such as NOBL vs FRDPX.

The major classifications of ETFs are 1. Simulating an index such as SPY, QQQ and DIA, 2. Simulating a sector such as XLE and SOXX, 3. Simulating an asset class such as GLD and SLV, 4. Simulating a country or a group of countries such as EWC and FXI, 5. Managed by a manager(s) such as ARKK, 6. Betting a market or sector to go down such as SH and PSQ, and 7. Leveraged (not recommended for beginners).

Fidelity: Index ETFs (https://www.fidelity.com/etfs/overview).

Wikipedia on ETF (http://en.wikipedia.org/wiki/Exchange-traded_fund).

List of ETFs
ETF database (Recommended): http://etfdb.com/
ETF Bloomberg: http://www.bloomberg.com/markets/etfs/
ETF Trends: http://www.etftrends.com/
A list of ETFs. Seeking Alpha.
http://etf.stock-encyclopedia.com/category/)
A list of contra ETFs (or bear ETFs)
http://www.tradermike.net/inverse-short-etfs-bearish-etf-funds/
Misc.: ETFGuide, ETFReplay
Fidelity low-cost index funds:
https://www.youtube.com/watch?v=zpKi4_IJvlY
Fidelity Annuity funds with performance data.
http://fundresearch.fidelity.com/annuities/category-performance-annual-total-returns-quarterly/FPRAI?refann=005

Other resources
Most subscription services offer research on ETFs. IBD has a strategy dedicated to ETFs and so does AAII to name a couple.

Seeking Alpha has extensive resources for ETF including an ETF screener and investing ideas. So is ETFdb.

Not all ETFs are created equal
Check their performances and their expenses.

When to use or not to use ETFs
I prefer sector mutual funds in some industries, as they have many bad stocks such as drug industry, banks, miners and insurers. Most mutual funds cannot time the market.

When you believe a sector is heading up (or contra ETF for heading down), but you do not have time to do research on specific stocks, buy an ETF for the sector; it is same for the market.

Half ETF
Taking out half of the stocks that score below the average in an index ETF could beat the same full ETF itself. I call it HETF (half the ETF). You heard it here first. To illustrate, sort the expected P/E (not including stocks with negative earnings) in ascending order and only include the stocks on the first half. Add more fundamental metrics. It will take a few minutes.

Disadvantages of ETFs
- When you have two stocks in a sector ETF one good one and one bad one, the ETF treats them the same. Stock pickers would buy the one that has a better appreciation potential.
- Sometimes the return could be misleading due to stock rotation. To illustrate this, on August 29, 2012, SHLD was replaced by LYB in a sector fund. SHLD was down by 4% and LYB was up by 4% primarily due to the switch. Unless you sell and buy at the right time (which is impossible), your return would not match the ETF's returns due to the replacement.
- Ensure the performance matches the corresponding index; it is hard due to excluding dividends.

Advantages of ETFs
- We have demonstrated that you can beat the market by using market timing. Between 2000 and Nov., 2013, you only exit and reenter the market 3 times and the result is astonishing.
- It is easy to rotate a sector vs. buying/selling all of the stocks in this sector. Rotating a sector is the same as trading a stock.
- The risk is spread out, and your portfolio is diversified especially for a market ETF or buying three or more ETFs in different sectors.
- Periodically the bad stocks in most funds are replaced by better stocks.
- Eliminate the time in researching stocks.

Leveraged ETFs

I do not recommend them. Some are 2x, 3x and even higher. They're too risky for beginners. However, when you are very sure or your tested strategy has very low drawdown, you may want to use them to improve performance. Most leveraged ETFs and contra ETFs have higher fees.

My basic ETF tables

I include some contra ETFs, mutual funds and Fidelity's annuity. Some of these may be interesting to you.

ETFs and funds come and go. Some ideas and classifications are my own interpretation. Refer to ETFdb for updated information. Not responsible for any error. Check out the ETF or fund before you take any action.

Table by market cap:

Category	ETF	Mutual Funds	Fidelity's Annuity	Contra ETF	Alternate
Size:					
Large Cap	DIA	See Blend		DOG	
	SPY			SH	FXAIX VOO
	QQQ			PSQ	FNCMX
	RYH				
Blend	IWD	BEQGX			
Growth	SPYG	FBGRX			FSPGX
Value	SPYV	DOGGX			FLCOX
Dividend	NOBL	FRDPX			
	VYM				
Mid Cap			FNBSC	MYY	
Blend	MDY	VSEQX			
Growth		STDIX			
		BPTRX			
Value		FSMVX			
Small Cap			FPRGC	SBB	FSSNX
Blend	IWM	HDPSX			
Growth		PRDSX			FECGX
Value		SKSEX			FISVX
Micro	IWC				

Multi						
Blend		VDEOX				
Growth		VHCOX				
Value		TCLCX				
Total						FSKAX
Bond						
Long Term (20)	VLV	BTTTX		TBF		
Mid Term (7 – 10)	VCIT	FSTGX				
Short Term (1 – 3 yrs.)	VCSH	THOPX				
Total	BOND	PONDX				
Corp Invest Grade	VCIT	NTHEX				
High Yield (junk)	PHB	SPHIX				
Muni	MUB	Check state				
Special situation						
Buy back	PKW					

Table by sectors:

Sector	ETF	Mutual Funds	Fidelity's Annuity
Banking[1]		FSRBK	
Regional	IAT		
Bio Tech	IBB	FBIOX	
	XBI	Large	
Consumer Dis.	XLY	FSCPX	FVHAC
Consumer Staple	XLP	FDFAX	FCSAC
Finance	KIE	FIDSX	FONNC
	IYF		
Energy	XLE	FSENX	FJLLC
Energy Service		FSESX	
Gold	GLD	FSAGX	
Gold Miner	GDX	VGPMX	
Health Care	IYH	FSPHX	FPDRC
	VHT	VGHCX	
House Builder	ITB	FSHOX	

	ITB	Perform	
Industrial	IYJ	FCYIX	FBALC
Material	VAW	FSDPX	
	IYM		
Oil	USO		
Oil Service	OIH	FSESX	
Oil Exploration	XOP		
Real Estate	VNQ	FRIFX	FFWLC
REIT	VNQ		
Retail	RTH	FSRPX	
	XRT		
Regional bank	KRE	FSRBX	
Semi Conduct	SMH		
Software	XSW	FSCSX	
	IGV		
Technology	XLK	FSPTX	FYENC
	FDN	FBSOX	
		ROGSX	
Telecomm.	VOX	FSTCX	FVTAC
Transport	XTN		
	IYT		
Utilities	XLU	FSUTX	FKMSC
Wireless		FWRLX	

Footnote. [1] Also check Finance.

Table by countries outside the USA:

Country	ETF	Mutual Funds	Fidelity's Annuity	Alternate
Australia	EWA			
Brazil	EWZ			
Canada	EWC	FICDX		
China	FXI	FHKCX		
EAFE	EFA			
Emerging	VWO	FEMEX	FEMAC	FPADX
Europe	VGK	FIEUX		
Global	KXI	PGVFX		
Greece	GREK			
India	INDY	MINDX		
Indonesia	EIDO			
Latin America	ILF	FLATX		
Nordic		FNORX		

Hong Kong	EWH		
Japan	EWJ	FJPNX	
S. Africa	EZA		
S. Korea	EWY	MAKOX	
Singapore	EWS		
Taiwan	EWT		
	TUR		
United Kingdom	EWU		
Foreign:			
Combination			
Intern. Div.	IDV		FTIHX
Small Cap	SCZ		
Value	EFV		
Europe	VGK		

#Filler: Honey, my book can play music.

https://www.youtube.com/watch?v=HxGT5z6d-GA&list=PLMZa6mP7jZ2b1otqG4tfbgZpLEdh6YiNF

It may cut down commercials by casting it to TV.

www.ingramcontent.com/pod-product-compliance
Lightning Source LLC
Chambersburg PA
CBHW051649170526
45167CB00001B/393